THE AUTHORS

TOM WILBER investigates documentation regarding U.S. detainees in the Democratic Republic of Việt Nam from 1964 until 1973. His research is the source for the 2015 Hà Nội National Film Festival award-winning documentary, *The Flower Pot Story*, produced by Ngọc Dũng. A visiting lecturer at Hà Nội University in 2018, his opinion pieces have been published in *Việt Nam News*. Wilber represents a U.S.–based nongovernmental organization that works on humanitarian projects with Vietnamese organizations.

JERRY LEMBCKE grew up in Northwest Iowa. He was drafted in 1968 and served as a chaplain's assistant in Vietnam. He is the author of eight books including *The Spitting Image, CNN's Tailwind Tail*, and *Hanoi Jane*. His opinion pieces have appeared in *The New York Times, Boston Globe*, and *The Chronicle of Higher Education*. He is Associate Professor of Sociology, Emeritus, at Holy Cross College, and Distinguished Lecturer for the Organization of American Historians.

From Vietnam's Hoa Lo Prison to America Today

Dissenting
POWs

Tom Wilber and Jerry Lembcke

MONTHLY REVIEW PRESS
New York

Library of Congress Cataloging-in-Publication data
available from the publisher

ISBN paper: 978-158367-908-1
ISBN cloth: 978-158367-909-8

Cover photo courtesy of Chu Chi Thanh; from Chu Chí Thành,
Memories of the War, (Hanoi: Vietnam News Agency Publishing
House, 2015).

Typeset in Minion Pro and Impact

MONTHLY REVIEW PRESS, NEW YORK
monthlyreview.org

5 4 3 2 1

Contents

Dedicated to Al Riate and Bob Chenoweth

*May their persistence in conscience and inspiration to others
while POWs encourage their successors in uniform
to perform with comparable integrity*

Former POWs Al Riate (left) and Bob Chenoweth
post-release in 1974 at Los Angeles International Airport
(photo provided by Bob Chenoweth)

Acknowledgments

Jerry is grateful for Tom Wilber's insight that the story of POW dissent needed to be written. His contribution to the book was accomplished with Tom's patience with his own impatience with IT and Carolyn Howe's help with online sourcing. Mike Yates and the Monthly Review Press team provided some best-ever editing.

Along with Jerry's appreciation for the Monthly Review team, Tom is grateful to Cora Weiss for encouragement and introductions, to Chuck Searcy for the suggestion to "talk to Jerry Lembcke," and to Jerry for listening carefully for the signal within the noise. Madame Nguyễn Thị Bích Thủy and Lê Đỗ Huy opened doors that led to unimaginable discoveries.

Introduction

On Memorial Day 2012, President Barack Obama called for the commemoration of Vietnam War events from 1961 to 1973 with these words: "Today begins the fiftieth commemoration of our war in Vietnam." The President's invitation inspired conferences, newspaper columns, and books recalling the 1965 landing of Marines at Danang and the campus teach-ins it spawned, the 1967 March on the Pentagon, and the 1968 My Lai Massacre. The documentary *The Vietnam War*, produced for public television by Ken Burns and Lynn Novick in 2017, brought interest in the war back to levels it had not had since the early postwar years.

Along with the Moratorium Days of 1969, the invasion of Cambodia and Kent State shootings of 1970, and the Christmas bombings of 1972, it is certain that interest in remembrances of the war will remain high through the fiftieth commemoration of the signing of Peace Accords in 2023, and beyond.

THE POW STORY

American prisoners of war (POWs) were made up of ground troops who were captured in South Vietnam and taken to Hanoi and pilots shot down over North Vietnam. They became critical figures in the negotiations that led to the end of the war—President Nixon insisting that U.S. troops would not be withdrawn from the South until the POWs were released, and the communist representatives insisting that there would be no prisoner return until the United States pulled out.

Concerned Americans of all political stripes rallied in support of the welfare of the POWs and in support of their families, anxious about the whereabouts of their loved ones. The Nixon administration, responding to the growing public concern for the POWs and having campaigned on a platform of ending the war, vaulted to the front of the growing parade, seizing the POW issue and weaponizing it as a negotiation lever to delay the war's end. The public responded with patriotic and humanistic concern for POW welfare. A California student group sold metal bracelets for a couple of dollars each with the POW's name, rank, and date of capture or disappearance etched on them; five million Americans bought the bracelets and vowed to wear them until the namesake returned or was accounted for. Businessman Ross Perot, to bring attention to the POW plight, bankrolled a chartered planeload of packages and mail to the captives. The Democratic Republic of Vietnam ended up refusing the shipment for logistical reasons, but Perot's effort proved to be a public relations victory, creating sympathy for the POWs and generating support for the hard line that the Nixon administration was taking in negotiations to end the war.[1]

Women Strike for Peace (WSP), meeting with the Vietnamese Women's Union in Toronto in 1969, began a process, women's group to women's group, to transport mail between POWs and their families at home in both directions, using delegations of peace activists as couriers. The WSP group returned just before Christmas 1969 with 138 letters from 132 prisoners and a provisional list of Americans held in Hanoi. Under the name Committee of Liaison with Families of Servicemen Detained in North Vietnam, the service delivered thousands of letters by the end of the war.[2]

After a gradual escalation in the late 1950s through 1964, the American war in Vietnam lasted nearly a decade, with massive increases beginning in 1965. The standard tour of duty for military personnel was twelve months, which meant there was a constant churn of those returning home and their newly deployed replacements. The country's emotions were divided: pride and elation for the returnees, grief for those who would never come home, worry for the wounded, and fear for those leaving for the war zone. With the comings and goings strung out for ages, emotions were uncentered when the Peace Accords were signed in January 1973. Many of the veterans had been home for years by the war's end, and troop levels had dwindled to less than 10 percent of the 1968 peak. These factors, when coupled with the war's loss, meant that welcome-home parades and their accoutrements were not in the offing—at least not until the POWs were released and returned in February and March of 1973.

Five hundred and ninety-one prisoners of war were released in the weeks following the Peace Accords that ended the war. The obscurity of the POWs' imprisonment and even questions about the survival of some of them lent an air of enchantment to the figures stepping off the planes at Clark Air Force Base. With bated breath, Americans of all persuasions anticipated the stories of the POWs' experience that would confirm the villainy of their captors and the strength of their own determination to return with honor, as affirmation of the goals seeded and nurtured by the Nixon administration since early 1969.

Dubbed "Operation Homecoming" by the Pentagon, the reception given the POWs surpassed anything mounted for previous generations of war veterans. Tickertape parades in New York City and Dallas produced the iconic scenes for returning warriors usually made in Hollywood; horn-honking caravans and marching bands typically accorded state-championship high school sports teams ushered POWs into small towns as conquering heroes; newspaper headlines kept the POWs in the spotlight for weeks. In May 1973, President Nixon welcomed them and their spouses to the White House in the largest reception of its type to date.

Theirs were cover-page portraits for all the major news magazines, their survival an allegory for the military victory otherwise denied, their return igniting triumphalist energies capped by years of disappointing news from the war front.

THE OTHER VOICES COMING HOME FROM HANOI

But amid the celebrations, there was discord. A March 16, 1973, *New York Times* headline announced, "Eight May Face Courts-Martial for Antiwar Roles as P.O.W.s." The eight enlisted men were accused of having expressed their opposition to the war while held as prisoners. Days later, one of two officers who would also face charges, Navy captain Gene Wilber (author Tom Wilber's father), shot down over North Vietnam in 1968, was grilled by journalist Mike Wallace for CBS's *60 Minutes* about the antiwar statements he had made. Had Wilber succumbed to torture? Or had his dissent been bought by prison guards for favorable treatment? Wilber parried Wallace's inferences and ended the interview saying his words had been sincere expressions of his "morality and conscience."

NEW SOURCES ON DISSENT WITHIN HOA LO PRISON

This book tells the untold story of POW dissent and develops the history of attempts to repress that dissent and purge it from public memory. Tom Wilber's interviews with more than a dozen former administrators, guards, and staff workers from the notorious "Hanoi Hilton" supplement primary documents he found on more than thirty investigative trips to Vietnam that support a challenge to conventional historical accounts of the POW experience and debunk the legends that have grown around it.

Chief among Tom Wilber's findings are POWs' handwritten reflections on their roles and the U.S. government's role in the conflict, letters from family members, texts for recording sessions by POWs broadcast on Radio Hanoi, some of which have been correlated to CIA-monitored transcripts of broadcasts matching those same documents, handwritten English-language training books and materials authored by prisoners, dozens of editorial cartoons by prisoners, and a range of international reading materials from the Hoa Lo prison library. On the basis of individual interviews of former detention camp staff, Wilber describes internal camp processes, including how statements were taken from prisoners, documented, recorded, and broadcast. From this research, he learned even the mundane routines of prison life, such as budgets, supply logistics, food procurement and preparation, and camp regulations.

CLASS: THE ROOTS OF DISSENT

The struggle between antiwar POWs and their Senior Ranking Officers involved the dissidents' conscientious objections to the war and their resistance to the controlling behavior of the SROs. The SROs saw their exercise of authority as legally vested in their rank and supported by their reading of the Code of Conduct. Threatening POW dissenters with courts-martial for their acts after their release, the SROs were able to intimidate them enough to ply the news media with their version of imprisonment, a version that became known as the "official story."

Left that way in the existing literature, the story of conflict among the POWs is understandable with conventional models of organizational behavior—for example, the labor-management relations common to most workplaces—tempered with the range of political and social values specific to war and military service.

In *Dissenting POWs*, however, we pursue a hunch that the tensions between POWs were rooted in the disparate socioeconomic backgrounds of the antagonists. The privileged backgrounds of the SROs were in sharp contrast with the modest origins of war resisters. It's a hunch triggered by clues scattered by Craig Howes in his 1993 book *Voices of the Vietnam POWs,* and reinforced in Milton Bates's 1996 *The Wars We Took to Vietnam.* We use newly available biographical and oral history material to show that class disparities extended into the SRO ranks. Objections to the war voiced by two of the most senior officers, Gene Wilber and Edison Miller, got them banished by their peers.

CLASS: A DISCOURSE FOR STIGMATIZING
AND DISPLACING DISSENT

Just as "class" designates an objective social position with implications for wealth and income and values derived from its material realities, it also connotes the subjective evaluations that members of one class make of others. Modifiers like "upper" and "lower" class imply character and even moral judgments that are then arranged, even if unwittingly, into hierarchies for assigning social standing and status.

The first substantial history of the POW experience, John Hubbell's *P.O.W.: A Definitive History of the American Prisoner-of-War Experience in Vietnam, 1964–1973*, records that the SROs viewed the antiwar expressions of their POWs within a class framework: the rebels were from poor or broken families, less educated than themselves, and of weaker personal character. The "weak character" rap against the antiwar captives was a way to dismiss the authenticity of their political views, a form of "psychologizing the political" that *Dissenting POWs* will show was integral as well to the way that GI and veteran dissent was being categorized stateside.

The mental health discourse deployed by the SROs against their comrades in confinement had been prototyped in Albert Biderman's 1963 *March to Calumny: The Story of American POWs in the Korean War* and would come to dominate the narrative of POWs returned from Hanoi in early 1973.

SILENCING DISSENT: POWERS OF STATE, MEDIA,
AND NARRATIVE

Even the best histories of U.S. prisoners of war in Vietnam, books by Michael J. Allen, Elliot Gruner, H. Bruce Franklin, and Natasha Zaretsky, give slight attention to the story of dissidents within the POW population, and even less attention to why public memory of those voices is lost. In *Dissenting POWs* we restore to proper prominence the record of antiwar voices within the POW population. We cull from the existing literature the role of government and Pentagon censorship in suppressing the story, and the role of Hollywood in eliding altogether the presence of antiwar POWs from its scripts and otherwise milking their story for its entertainment value à *la* the Rambo series and POW-rescue films.

However, we argue that the public memory of dissenting POWs was lost less to censoring or the demands of the movie market than it was to displacement of their acts of principled courage by images of them as victims of the war. Casting POW dissenters as sadsack losers precluded their inclusion in the great American captivity narrative at the center of the nation's founding mythology, wherein the captive-hero remains a prisoner *at* war, loyal to the mission on which he was sent. The antiwar Vietnam POWs would be the antiheroes in, say, the legend of John Smith and his resolve in the face of torture and the temptations of Pocahontas—the weakling POWs had no place in the American story, no association with traditions out of which memories could have been constructed.

The *coup de grâce* to American memory of the POW experience was dealt by the rumors that some POWs had been left behind when the United States departed Vietnam. The conspiratorial threads in those stories had it that prisoners had been knowingly abandoned by shadowy sell-out forces within the U.S. government that settled the war on terms favorable to international communism. *Dissenting POWs* delves into the post–Vietnam War POW-MIA fantasies that echoed the Cold War hysteria about brainwashing and prisoner defections.

The banishment of POW dissent from memory leaves a void in American political culture where new generations of uniformed war resisters will look for role models, and civilian activists will look for allies in their efforts to end U.S. wars of aggression. Filling that void is the mission of this book.

1

Forgotten Voices from Hoa Lo Prison: Dissent in the Hero-Prisoner Story

At first glance, the history of U.S. POWs in Vietnam appears to be an exercise in hero construction, a story of prisoners remaining loyal to their mission and one another. Many of their memoirs record the resistance of shot-down pilots to efforts at extracting sensitive information from them in return for better medical care, food, and early release.[1] When they defied their captors, some of the POWs say they were tortured until they complied. The hero-prisoner was a holdout who sacrificed his own comfort rather than divulging information that might put his comrades, in the air or field, at greater risk or even compromise the security of the American homeland.[2]

The hardcore holdout-POW is the central figure in the history of the American version of the Vietnam War POW experience that historian Craig Howes sarcastically dubbed the "Official Story."[3] The official story appeared in print in 1976 as *P.O.W.: A Definitive History of the American Prisoner of War Experience in Vietnam, 1964–1973.* The book was a project of *Reader's Digest,* proposed to author John G. Hubbell by the magazine's managing editor, Kenneth O. Gilmore, who gave him a "blank check" for the work.[4] The Pentagon assigned its public affairs chief, Jerry Friedheim, to assist Hubbell. Friedheim also had key roles in managing the Operation Homecoming messaging and granting access to former POWs for interviews and press releases, as well as managing information requests from congressional staffs related to POWs changing their stories from fair treatment to torture after their release. Hubbell's *P.O.W.* also had the imprimatur of Admiral Thomas H. Moorer, the Chairman of the Joint Chiefs of Staff (JCS), virtually ensuring that *P.O.W.* would reflect the interests of the military establishment. Nobody was more establishment than Moorer and nobody had a greater stake in the way the POW story would be told. He was Chief of Naval Operations from 1967 to 1970, during which time, in '68 and '69, 116 Americans were captured, many of them Navy pilots.

Moorer became Chairman of the Joint Chiefs on July 1, 1970, and assumed control of one of the most controversial and secretive operations of the entire war—the POW rescue raid on Son Tay in North Vietnam where it was thought as many as seventy U.S. prisoners were held. Son Tay, about 23 miles west of Hanoi, was one of several POW holding centers in the Hanoi region. The Vietnamese designated each of them by number and Son Tay was T142. The American POWs coined nicknames for many of the sites, such as Briarpatch, Zoo, and Skid Row. Only the central prison, Hoa Lo, was known as the "Hanoi Hilton," though it, too, was sectioned off with POW nicknames such as New Guy Village, Camp Unity, Little Vegas, and Heartbreak.

Son Tay had been under aerial surveillance for weeks when Moorer took over as JCS chairman, and planning for the raid was already underway. The plan called for about fifty Special Forces troops to launch by multiple helicopters from Thailand, led by sophisticated slow-flying navigation aircraft, to fly over Laos and land inside the prison compound. The operation involved in-flight refueling of the helicopters and the support of fighter-bombers providing cover for the raiders. A sea-launched bombing raid on Hanoi would divert attention from the attack on Son Tay, twenty-three miles west of the city. Training for the mission, costing millions of dollars, had taken place over several months at Eglin Air Force Base in Florida. The raiding party was made up of some of the war's most decorated soldiers, including the legendary Green Berets Bull Simons and Dick Meadows.

The raiders set off on the night of November 20, 1970, but the mission was a failure with a comedic flare. Intelligence failures were evident from the outset, including misjudging the density and the height of trees at Son Tay, which differed from the trees at their practice site. One chopper crashed after hitting a tree; Bull Simons's team of twenty-two men landed at a secondary school a quarter-mile south of the target; and, if that was not enough, Son Tay was empty of prisoners—there were no POWs there.[5] Hubbell began work for his book hand-in-hand with Pentagon insiders at the very time Moorer was enmeshed in the scandal over who was responsible for the Son Tay debacle and the conspiratorial speculations that led to it. The book's Acknowledgments say Hubbell asked for Moorer's "support and *guidance*" (emphasis added) in the writing and a few sentences later repeated the words saying Moorer's support and guidance were "forthcoming in unstinting measure." The suggestion in those words of Hubbell's subservience to the Pentagon's need for a whitewashed POW history gains confirmation in the book's later assessment of the Son Tay raid as "a huge success."

I like people who weren't captured.
—DONALD TRUMP

Donald Trump is responding here to Arizona senator John McCain, who had earlier expressed his own skepticism of Trump's suitability for the presidency. The campaigns for the 2016 elections were just getting underway, and McCain supporters had been invoking the senator's record as a fighter pilot and POW during the war in Vietnam. McCain's five and a half years as a prisoner in the legendary Hanoi Hilton, they said, made him an American hero. Trump's retort made headlines on July 18, 2015, because of its use for campaign leverage, but it was a line he had been using for years.[6]

The centrality of the POW story to American remembrance of the war in Vietnam and the competing narratives it helps construct could not be made clearer than does this give-and-take between candidate Trump and Senator McCain's supporters. The image of pilots shot out of the sky, captured and rendered helpless, and ground troops taken prisoner and held in bamboo cages, were symbolic of the lost war itself. Their confinement symbolized the inferiority of the U.S. military men and machines, and the humiliation they faced on the international stage. It was exactly the imagery that Moorer and the *Reader's Digest* team had in mind, and which they wanted expunged from memory, when they commissioned John Hubbell to create the alternative "official" story out of the actual facts of shot-down pilots and captive GIs.

The hero-prisoner story would portray the prison experience as, in a sense, another war front, another theater-of-war, in which the POWs fought gallantly "behind enemy lines" and came out on top as hero-warriors. Carrier air wing commander James Stockdale (promoted after captivity to admiral rank) who was shot down on September 9, 1965, fit this profile. As a carrier air group commander who chose to fly a mission on that fateful day, Stockdale was the highest-ranking officer captured. Described by Craig Howes[7] as "one of the Navy's 'princes of the realm, the blood Royal,'" he had graduated from the Naval Academy and gotten a master's degree in international relations at Stanford University. At Stanford, he had learned how U.S. POWs had been brainwashed during the Korean War. Now, he made the association in his mind: the Vietnamese guards' compassionate treatment of captives while "educating" them on the history of the Vietnamese independence movement was an attempt at mind control. As the senior officer among the POW population, his enforcement of noncompliance among his more junior POWs had to be absolute.[8]

Hubbell did return to the brainwashing theme later in the book when describing the hard line that SROs (Senior Ranking Officers) like Stockdale were taking against their own, lower-ranking, fellow captives. However, he didn't belabor it. He may have assumed that mere references to brainwashing were sufficient given the historical closeness, at the time, of Americans to their Korean War experience. Moreover, the 1962 film *The Manchurian Candidate* starring Frank Sinatra, Janet Leigh, and Angela Lansbury had lodged into American imaginations the image of a brainwashed POW returning from Korea as a communist sleeper agent.[9]

Stockdale had command-level company in Navy Commander (later Rear Admiral) Jeremiah Denton Jr. and Air Force Lieutenant Colonel (later Brigadier General) Robinson Risner. Denton was a squadron executive officer shot down on July 18 and like Stockdale was a product of the Naval Academy with a master's degree, his in international relations from Georgetown. In his memoir *When Hell Was in Session*, he writes of his parents' pride in their "Southern aristocratic background" and touts his own expertise in airborne electronics, antisubmarine warfare, and air defense. He assessed himself a "good catch" for the North Vietnamese. Risner had been shot down just days after Stockdale and entered the prison system as a bona fide American hero: a Korean War ace and test pilot, he had set a transatlantic speed record flying the anniversary Lindbergh flight in 1957 and had been rescued after being shot down over North Vietnam months earlier. However, unlike the service academy "royals" Stockdale and Denton, Risner, son of a sharecropper, entered the Army during the Second World War after high school and trained for two years to become a pilot, at which point he was commissioned a second lieutenant and served out the remainder of the war in Panama, leaving the military after the war, while maintaining his flying skills with the Oklahoma Air National Guard. He was recalled to active duty in 1951 after hostilities broke out in Korea.

Fortunately for Stockdale, Denton, and Risner, whom Craig Howes would later dub, sardonically, "the triumvirate of great leaders," they were handed Navy Lieutenant Junior Grade Rodney Knutson, a radar intercept officer, shot down with pilot Ralph Gaither on October 17, 1965. The peculiar circumstances of Knutson's capture were fitting for the three to begin confecting a chain of command within the prison population that ran parallel to that of the North Vietnamese prison

administration. Later acknowledging its "Mickey Mouse" appear-
ance, they imagined the hierarchy they desired being justified if not
required by the U.S. Military Code of Conduct for POWs.

In retrospect, the made-up chain of command may have been a
function of the SROs' authoritarian personalities—their psychological need to subordinate others—or as a ruse to manage the theatrics
of the prisoner-*at*-war narrative they wanted performed. By the time
of Knutson's arrival, Stockdale, Denton, and Risner had already abandoned their tough-guy holdout postures and made compromising
statements to their Vietnamese interrogators. They said they had
been tortured into talking. But had they? The question would never
be asked if all the later-arriving captives, beginning with Knutson,
could tell the same story. Thusly reasoned, notification of the chain
of command was disseminated through the prison along with the
order from the top that *all* prisoners should be like the Great Three
and submit to torture before making statements beyond the name,
rank, and serial number protocol. In the end, pressures to meet the
expectations of the SROs led to behavior that *invited* torture to avoid
post-release charges for collaboration upon release.

RODNEY KNUTSON: A PRISONER *AT* WAR

Hubbell found the model for his still-in-the-fight captive in Navy
Lieutenant Junior Grade Rodney Knutson. In Hubbell's account,
Knutson was the first shot-down pilot to have exchanged gunfire with
his Vietnamese captors. Hubbell wrote that Knutson had fired a tracer
round from his .38 caliber pistol into the head of a Vietnamese militia-
man, and a round at point-blank range at another before blacking out.
Then taken to Hanoi by "a small army contingent," he was assaulted
along the way by villagers who were egged on by an officer with a bull-
horn.[10] At Hoa Lo, he then refused to cooperate in the questioning by
interrogators beyond the standard practice of giving his name, rank,
and serial number—Knutson was a prisoner, but not out of action.

Knutson's description in *P.O.W.* of his conditions of incarceration
at Hoa Lo was unpleasant to put it mildly: distasteful food, endless

interrogations, and rats. His description of the rats, some as large as small dogs that crawled close to his face, is graphic and chilling. But his description of the physical abuse he is meted takes readers into new territory: lying on his stomach, a length of clothesline rope was looped around his arms just above the elbow then pulled and cinched until circulation was cut off. With his elbows tied together, he was made to sit with his ankles locked into stocks at the foot of the bed. He was then ordered to apologize for "insulting the Vietnamese," and when he didn't, he was then beaten until his nose and several teeth were broken.

The brutalizing of Knutson continues for five pages of *P.O.W.*, completing, thereby, the book's transition to the first of the torture allegations that is the centerpiece of the prisoner-at-war narrative. Knutson was the first of several POWs "going to the ropes," as they phrased it.[11]

But was it torture, or punishment? The answer is a matter of the guards' motivation or intent. By Hubbell's telling, Knutson had refused to eat his dinner and dumped it into a waste bucket and then refused to apologize. Hubbell quotes Knutson as being told: "For insulting the Vietnamese people . . . you must be punished."[12] Rule 10 of "Camp Regulations" posted in each cell was: "Violations of the regulations shall be punished." Was the wasteful act of throwing away a meal a prison discipline problem?

It is curious, however, that POW refusals to eat had been routine since the first pilot taken captive. Lieutenant Junior Grade Everett Álvarez had arrived fifteen months earlier. Alvarez had flown off the carrier USS *Constellation* on August 5, 1964, in an A4 Skyhawk over the Tonkin Gulf along the coast of Vietnam. After strafing a North Vietnamese patrol boat, his plane was hit and he parachuted into the waters of Ha Long Bay some sixty kilometers east-northeast of Haiphong. Álvarez was plucked from the water by Vietnamese in a small boat and wrapped in rope "like a top" wrote Hubbell. Some of his captors screamed at him and kicked him. "Certain that he was about to be hanged by his ankles, skinned, relieved of his testicles and finally his head," he was transferred to a torpedo boat and taken to shore. On August 11, he was transported by jeep to Hoa Lo prison in Hanoi.[13]

As the first of a population that would eventually grow, although slowly at first, to nearly 600, Álvarez was likely unaware that his captors had no plan what to do with him. With a captured pilot in transport to Hanoi, the army went to the Hanoi police to ask for space in Hoa Lo Prison, at that time a civil jail administered by the city. The police gave the army some empty offices initially to use as prison cells, and then "four or five" actual cells in one section of the prison. Eventually the police transferred control of Hoa Loa to the army, but until kitchen facilities were available, the army guards went to local restaurants to buy carry-out for the initial prisoners.[14]

Still, as described in *P.O.W.*, Álvarez's prison conditions were unpleasant. Some of the meals—chicken heads, a cow hoof, animal hair, and shrimp with eyes in—he left uneaten; others he vomited up. He fed interrogators only misinformation, and yet they only played on his fears of never going home—there were no ropes for him.

So why would the Knutson incident have called forth more severe measures? Why now? Why him? Was his punishment really for insulting the Vietnamese by wasting their food and then refusing to apologize? What about the two Vietnamese militia people he had shot and maybe killed? It makes sense that someone be "sent to the ropes" as *punishment* for a crime like murder, as the Vietnamese may have viewed the shootings. But "ropes" for rudeness seems like an excuse for meanness—torture—which is the essential ingredient in the prisoner-at-war story that Hubbell is writing. Might it be the case, then, that Hubbell switched-out the criminal indictment for one of insensitivity and defiance? Hubbell's hero-prisoner story is riddled with incongruities like these.

It's probable as well that the torture spin on Knutson's story was already part of the camp lore that elevated into a canon in the hero-prisoner myth/legend that would be brought back from Hanoi by the SROs in 1973, rather than something that Hubbell created. Knutson's obstinance and toughness were, after all, exactly the traits that Stockdale could point to in October 1965 as the standard that all the captives should meet—Knutson embodied the prisoner-at-war ethic. When the two met on October 29, Stockdale supposedly said to Knutson, "I think you did a fine job, Rob . . . you took the right approach. Give them nothing, make them take it from you."[15]

Stockdale's adoption of Knutson as his prisoner-at-war poster-boy was not without complications. It was against international law for Knutson to have shot a tracer round at an enemy. Years later, he acknowledged thinking, at the moment of shooting, that he could get in trouble for it.[16] Stockdale, as his prison SRO, either didn't know about the shooting—it's possible that Knutson didn't tell him—or was complicit in reconfiguring the punishment-for-crime story (or discipline-for-breaking-camp-rules-by-wasting-food story) into the torture-for-resistance story more useful for the prisoner-at-war role he had in mind for Knutson.[17]

In covering the eighteen months after the Knutson incident, *P.O.W.* is a compilation of shoot downs, backgrounds of the pilots, the stories of their capture and transport to Hanoi, descriptions of the appalling conditions of their confinement, their despair at never going home, the endless interrogations, and the torture they suffered for refusing to answer the questions and refusing to apologize for not answering.

WRINKLES IN THE HERO-PRISONER STORY

The united front of the prisoners-at-war in Hoa Lo faced its first challenge in the spring of 1967 when news of the stateside antiwar movement reached their eyes and ears. The April 15 demonstrations across the country had brought together labor, religious, SDS (Students for a Democratic Society), and civil rights groups to oppose the war. Known as Spring Mobe, short for the Spring Mobilization to End the War in Vietnam, the effort turned out 400,000 protesters in New York City and 75,000 in San Francisco. The success of the Mobe also spurred the organizing of resistance within the military. Bus terminals like the New York's Port Authority, through which hundreds of GIs passed daily, became centers of protester outreach to military personnel. Some military members, like Private Howard Petrick stationed at Fort Hood in Texas, took the radical literature of the civilian activists into their barracks for distribution to their buddies. A year later, those efforts blossomed into a network of underground antiwar newspapers written and printed by and for GIs, Marines, sailors, and airmen.

Hoa Lo administrators made sure that news of the growing homefront opposition to the war reached the prison inmates.[18] Hubbell wrote that prison staff had POWs read newspaper reports of the demonstrations to their fellow captives over the intercom. They all heard the news that political and religious leaders were condemning the war: Martin Luther King Jr. calling it "blasphemy"; Dr. Benjamin Spock expressing "scorn and horror" for it; Nobel Prize–winner Dr. Linus Pauling feeling "shame" for the war. Hubbell wrote that POWs "felt bewildered, depressed, betrayed. They understood political leaders dissenting from policy and opposing it, but not openly opposing it to the enemy's benefit while the country was still at war."[19]

Although Hubbell presents it as such, news of the Spring Mobe would not have been shocking to the POWs. The prison administration regularly made U.S. news magazines like *Time* and *Newsweek* available to the prisoners, and those publications were full of antiwar news even before the 1967 Mobe. In November 1965, Norman Morrison, a Quaker opposed to the war for religious reasons, immolated himself outside the Pentagon office of Defense secretary Robert McNamara. On March 26, 1966 (Sunday March 27, 1966), the *New York Times* ran a striking front-page visual pairing a photograph of Marines going ashore in Vietnam with a photograph of the antiwar march. The caption atop the two photos read: "Marines Land South of Saigon—Marchers Protest Policy on Vietnam." The Bertrand Russell Tribunal had convened in Stockholm in December 1966 to consider allegations of war crimes committed by the United States. Historians Stuart Rochester and Frederick Kiley say the POWs knew about the Morrison immolation and the Russell Tribunal.[20]

Additionally, pilots shot down after March 1965 when teach-ins against the war had begun on college campuses would themselves have been exposed to the growing unpopularity of the war; many of them, after all, would have been students on those campuses. In October 1967, a delegation of peace activists from the United States met with prisoners in Hanoi. One of them, Air Force captain Larry Carrigan, was asked about his knowledge of demonstrations in the States:

> Sure, we knew; at Flight School there were two guys from Berkeley who told us about demonstrations. We figured it was something to do on a Saturday afternoon, get together and paint a sign. I remember Econ class, the guy used to sit next to me, all of a sudden next week he wasn't there, got drafted, it got you thinking.[21]

Not surprisingly, then, the later shoot downs arrived with "long hair, sideburns, beards and mustaches," styles that may have suggested an affinity with the stateside antiwar and counterculture movements that was unnerving when seen by those already in Hoa Lo.[22]

Indeed, military personnel and veterans were becoming prominent in the antiwar movement by late 1965. A November 24, 1965, advertisement in the *New York Times* sponsored by the Ad Hoc Committee of Veterans for Peace in Vietnam had excoriated the November 1965 fight for the Ia Drang Valley in which 237 Americans and 1,200 North Vietnamese had been killed. In July 1966, the refusal of three GIs at Fort Hood to report for shipment to Vietnam made news across the country.

Finally, direct contact with American peace activists visiting Hoa Lo would have alerted POWs to the escalating opposition to the war at home. In August 1965 at the World Peace Congress in Helsinki, W. E. B. Du Bois Club members, student and civil rights activist Harold Supriano, Du Bois Club international secretary Michael Myerson, WBAI-FM program director Jon Christopher Koch, and freelance writer Richard Ward were invited to come to Hanoi in the fall at the invitation of the Vietnamese delegates.[23] In the fall of 1965 these members of the American antiwar W. E. B. Du Bois club visited Hoa Lo and met with American POW Air Force captain Robert Daughtrey[24] from Texas who had been captured in August. In

December 1965, Professors Herbert Aptheker and Staughton Lynd, along with SDS president Tom Hayden, were invited to Hanoi by the North Vietnamese through the World Peace Congress. Aptheker said they "interviewed" an Air Force POW of five months, who had been shot down "on (his) first mission,"[25] and returned to the States with letters he had written to his family.[26]

The POWs who met with the peace travelers may have been the forerunners of a larger group that would emerge later to speak out against the war and resist the authority of the SROs. And there may have been more than two peace-leaning prisoners at the time. Hubbell, after all, makes no mention of Daughtrey's meeting with the Du Bois delegation and does not mention any meeting of POWs with the Aptheker group. Might he have left out other early instances of POWs conversing with antiwar activists?

Hubbell doesn't tell of the early meetings of antiwar visitors with POWs, but when he does tell of those events, he suggests that the prisoners were forced to do it by the guards.[27] His explanation that it was coercion, rather than prisoners' own belief, may have been correct. But many more prisoner-activist meetings would occur in the coming years, and historians writing in the postwar years were skeptical of the idea that they were all coerced.[28] The stories, for example, that POWs were forced to meet actor and activist Jane Fonda when she visited Hanoi in 1972 have been discredited as attempts to discount the sincerity of the POWs and vilify her and the Vietnamese. On the other hand, when coupled with Hubbell's omission of previous instances of prisoner meetups with peace activists, such as the Du Bois group, it is also possible that he was manufacturing a case, inferentially at least, that dissent was not indigenous to the prison population itself and appeared only later when media reports, biased against the war, began leaking into camp.

DISSENT BREAKS OUT IN HOA LO

Hubbell writes that by 1971 "at least 30 percent and perhaps as many as 50 percent of the prisoners were disillusioned about the war and becoming increasingly cynical about it."[29] Left at that, the numbers seem to contradict the central narrative of the hero-prisoner myth/legend, the "official story" that the POWs remained *at* war until they returned home with honor at the bitter end. For Hubbell, however, the numbers provide confirmation of two contaminating externalities at work in the culture of the prison population: the pervasive use of torture as a kind of conversion therapy by the prison guards, and the arrival in Hanoi in 1971 of U.S Army and Marine Corps ground troops who had been taken prisoner in the South and whose mental and physical capabilities made them more susceptible to communist propaganda and mind control techniques.

"LIKE 95% OF THE POWs, I WAS TORTURED MANY TIMES."[30]

The prisoner *at* war is the central figure in the hero-prisoner story, and the experience of *torture* provides the validation that what went on in the Hanoi prison system was a form of war. The credibility of the narrative hinged on the verity of the torture claims. Postwar studies raised serious questions about the claims, and the interpolation of those questions, in turn, sheds light on the origins of dissent within Hoa Lo.

One question mark on the pervasiveness of torture has long been the absence of a comprehensive account of the POW experiences. The Vietnamese always denied using torture, and despite the political realignments, defections, and emigration that have characterized Vietnam in the postwar years, no former guards or prison administrators have corroborated the charges of the former POWs. Instead of corroboration, we have a London *Times* story of October 25, 2008, for which the reporter sought out Tran Trong Duyet, the former prison director, to ask about the claim by 2008 presidential candidate John McCain that he had been tortured as a prisoner in Hanoi. Duyet said, "I never tortured or mistreated the POWs nor did my staff." Nguyen Tien Tran, another director, confirmed Duyet, saying, "We had a clear code of taking care of the injured. Why would [McCain] say he was tortured?" The prison guards do not deny physical discipline, and they point to rules violations or responses to violent outbursts of anger or frustrations by the prisoners as reasons to administer physical discipline. When asked specifically why then would former prisoners report that they were tortured, even contradicting their statements otherwise, Nguyen Minh Y, retired camp administrator, replied that "people are opportunists."[31]

The former prison director's disavowal of torture certainly can be dismissed as self-serving, but in the absence of documentary evidence that torture *did* happen, the only "record" of it is the memories of the prisoners themselves, a record marked by their own self-interest in maintaining the realism of torture in the hero-prisoner-at-war narrative. But the remembered version has too much variation to be reliable. Almost all accounts agree that there was no torture after 1969, which means that any accounts of the 156 flyers shot down after January 1, 1970 (about a quarter of the POWs that returned in February and March 1973) is marginal to the prisoner-at-war story. There is a similar marker on the early years. The twenty-three pilots shot down during the first year of the air war over the North reported that they were not tortured until September 1965, after which some say they were and some say they were not, and most have remained silent on the issue. That discrepant pattern continues through the fall of 1969, raising questions about the reliability of the reports and the reasons for the variation of the memories.

Claims of torture are also countered by civilian visitors to the prison. Carol McEldowney, an American, was there in 1967 at the supposedly peak period of torture. She wrote in her journal that the "decent treatment" of prisoners had been verified and was no longer an issue. The objection that McEldowney was an advocate for ending the war and therefore biased against U.S. policy is itself countered by other writing in her journal. She wrestled with her own bias. Calling some of the North Vietnamese presentations on non-POW matters "bullshit" and "propaganda," she was, if anything, predisposed to believe the opposite of what her observations were telling her about the POWs' conditions.[32]

There is also disparity in the memories of POWs from different branches of service: of the seventy-five Army POWs who came home in 1973, all captured before 1970, forty tell their stories in the collection *We Came Home*, edited by Barbara Powers Wyatt, but none describes having been tortured. This is not to say that some of them were not treated badly. Gustav Mehrer, for example, described having been bound and hung by his arms during interrogation, but his report was an exception and he did not refer to it as torture. Army Major William Hardy made a point of saying he had *not* been tortured. George Smith's story is not in the Wyatt volume, but he wrote in his own book that he had been treated well by the National Liberation Front (NLF), known in the United States as the Viet Cong, literally "Vietnamese Communist," in the South. At the very least, this variegated picture dispels the claim made by Hubbell in his *P.O.W.* that torture was a systematic, day-to-day policy of the Vietnamese.

As an example of the inconsistencies in the treatment narratives, David Wesley Hoffman's story is a case study. Hoffman was interviewed by George Wald on February 19, 1972, less than two months after his capture. Wald was a Harvard professor, peace activist, and Nobel Prize winner for medical research. Hoffman was effusive in the details of his medical care for the compound fracture of his arm from his ejection. It was an obvious topic for discussion as Hoffman's immobilized arm projected horizontally from a cast that hospital doctors had specially configured to correctly heal his compound fracture of the humerus. Wald asked about his treatment when captured by local people:

GW: Did they treat you all right?

DH: They took me into their village and immediately got medical treatment. It was obvious to them I was hurt and they went and got the local doctor to come. It was a woman as a matter of fact. She strapped my arm, put a temporary splint on the thing and fixed it so that it wouldn't move so that when I was transported in, it was immobile, so that I didn't have problems there. They

fed me, gave me warm food, a good place for shelter, and treated
me very well.

GW: Doesn't it surprise you that they treated you so well?

DH: I was amazed, frankly and honestly. I didn't know what to expect,
honestly. But I was amazed, and I have been constantly and con-
tinually amazed at the treatment. From the time I was shot down
until this very moment my treatment has been superb.

After some back and forth discussion why the United States should
end the war and Hoffman's hope that Americans will elect a president
who can end it, the conversation went back to his arm:

DH: I'm not sure whether my arm hit part of the aircraft when we
ejected out of it, or whether we were going so fast that the wind
blast caused the injury. I had no other injury, there was just the
fracture of the left arm.

GW: It's the upper bone?

DH: Right up in here, yes sir, right up in the middle. The doctors
seem pretty satisfied that when they do take the cast off, that
I'll have full use of the arm and that everything will be all right
again. From what I've seen of the medical treatment—and that's
another thing—medical treatment. One of the doctors comes
every other day and checks on us to make sure we're perfectly all
right. For instance, I was having a problem with my hand when
I go to sleep, the hand would droop and go to sleep. I'd wake
up in the morning with it stiff. So today they brought me this
(showing a little, wrapped paddle that slipped into the end of his
splint) and it holds the hand up; and now when I go to sleep the
hand stays straight and doesn't cut the blood off. They are constantly concerned and checking on us. They feed us more than
we can eat.

Hoffman expounded more to Wald on the "very good" food and
eating "better than the guards who guard us."

Were these talking points required by his captors, it is hard to imagine a better acting performance: Hoffman's extemporaneous offering of information to Wald's unrehearsed questions seem to reinforce his belief in his own words.

With similar conviction, Hoffman joined eight other captured pilots in signing an April 1972 statement to the U.S. Congress objecting to a recent escalation of bombing. Asked during a May video interview to reiterate the substance of that statement, he said the bombings were a danger to the POWs that would also likely lengthen their imprisonment and were an ineffective means to dampen Vietnamese spirits. He made an eloquent call for peace and return to peace talks and, with other prisoners, met with actress and peace activist Jane Fonda in July 1972.

Despite his firm, clear, and seemingly voluntary discussion in multiple interviews as a prisoner, Hoffman changed his story after he returned to tell how he was forced to make these interviews and statements and that he had been physically coerced to meet with Wald. "I reject everything I said," Hoffman said in a press conference.[33]

In response, Wald submitted his documentation of the inconsistencies to Senator J. William Fulbright, who in turn inquired of the Department of Defense. In a letter of response Jerry W. Friedheim, who provided government-funded staff support and resources to the development of Hubbell's book *P.O.W.*, said that "the circumstances surrounding interviews conducted in captivity inside North Vietnam were considerably different from those in this country when the men were free." Friedheim's letter seemed to close the matter of these inconsistencies. It seems Wald's inquiry into Hoffman's inquiry ended there. Naval Academy graduate Hoffman continued his career, eventually commanding the aircraft carrier USS *Kitty Hawk* and retiring at the rank of captain.

The most objective data we have bearing on the treatment of the POWs is the 1975 Amnesty International report that the mental and physical condition of the POWs was "really good" when they arrived at Clark Air Base in the Philippines. The report was reinforced by a 1978 study that found former POWs to be in better health than a control group of non-captive Vietnam veterans, and a later study

showed them with fewer physical and psychological health problems
than POWs from previous wars. Furthermore, memoirs written by
POWs after post-traumatic stress disorder (PTSD) was included in
the *Diagnostic and Statistical Manual* (DSM) as a diagnostic category
make no mention of it and make only a few random references to
trauma.

> *Wilber and Miller delivered these offerings as though*
> *they were their own original ideas; it was apparent that they*
> *believed the things they were saying.*[34]
>   —JOHN G. HUBBELL

If a third to a half of the POWs were disillusioned with the war by
1971, the official account constructed by Hubbell contended that it
was the mind-altering viciousness of the torture the downed pilots
endured that made them vulnerable to North Vietnamese propaganda. The torture explanation for the dissent was complicated,
however, by the presence in the Hanoi holdings, by then, of the Army
and Marine ground troops and helicopter crews captured in the
South. As a group, they were even more opposed to the war despite
not having been tortured, and, as it would turn out, even less agree-
able to the prisoner-at-war roles in which Stockdale and the SROs
wanted to cast them.

The captives taken in the South were mostly enlisted personnel,
not officers. They were younger, with less formal education than most
of the pilots shot down over the North. The social distance between
the SROs and the enlisted men was a good predictor of who would be
a dissident. One dimension of that was the military hierarchy itself.
John Young, one of the enlisted men captured in the South and eventually moved to Hanoi, later recalled that "many of the enlisted men
opposed the war," a point that made sense given that a cross-section
of enlistees across the military were growing restive about the war by
the late 1960s and chafing under military authoritarianism. Enlisted
men, moreover, had less stake in the outcome of the war than did

officers whose military and political careers hinged on the success of their missions, notably senior officers, or those officers who were in a place in their careers beyond their initial commissioning obligations.

Those social status differences were intensified for the prisoner-at-war narrative by the greater contact that enlisted men had with the Vietnamese before their capture and during their days in jungle camps. Whereas officers, especially those flying off aircraft carriers—similarly Air Force officers flying from their American-style bases in Thailand—had never seen, much less interacted with, any Vietnamese before being shot down and meeting their enemy under the extraordinary circumstances of being captives. The enlisted men stationed on the ground in the South, however, are likely to have seen Vietnamese in more ordinary roles: street vendors, civilian employees on military installations, bar girls, or even girlfriends. Army soldiers would likely have been on a first-name basis with at least one Vietnamese and may have even known something about his or her family.

Captivity in the South would have exposed those Americans to the way the Vietnamese were experiencing the war. In his memoir *Black Prisoner of War*, James Daly recounts meeting the young volunteers working along the Ho Chi Minh Trail as he was moved by foot, truck, and train to the North:

> I'd seen or talked with a good number of Vietnamese. . . . They'd been peasants, Viet Cong, NVA soldiers, workers, professors, Montagnards. And the more Vietnamese I came in contact with, the more I knew in my gut . . . that the war was wrong, and we had no right to be tearing the country apart.[35]

Frank Anton, a chopper pilot downed in January 1968, recalled his treatment by an old Vietnamese woman after being captured:

> She saw my feet were wet. She removed my socks and dried my feet with a rag. She left and returned in a moment with a pair of clean white socks belonging to her. She pulled them very gently on my feet and hung mine up to dry. Other villagers had hissed

and thrown rocks at us as we passed. But this act of kindness was unexpected and I was touched.[36]

The cross-cultural exposure that GIs and Marines brought into Hoa Lo lent an element of humanity to the Vietnamese prison workers. Like the pilots shot down over the North, the men held in the South coined nicknames for their guards but were more likely to know their real names—Huong and Qua (a Montagnard), for example—and remember others respectfully years later as Mr. Ho or Mr. Bai.

It was the humanizing of the Other that the SROs seemed to fear the most, as if recognition of an element of "us" in "them" implied the obverse: the enemy within the hearts and minds of their own rank and file. The real fear, as Craig Howes put it, was of the "white gook," the POW underling who would give in to the urges of his inner-Other and emerge as an enemy-inside-the-gates. Believing that "enlisted men collaborated [with the enemy] almost instinctively,"[37] SROs viewed with alarm any behavior that looked Vietnamese to them— squatting or eating from a bowl, for example—as signs that one of their own may be crossing over. As prophylactic to cultural con- tamination, SROs enforced their own segregation of POWs from the Vietnamese, prohibiting, for example, their learning of the language.

THE RAID ON THE SON TAY prison camp in late 1970 was foiled by the movement of the POWs held there into facilities closer to the Hoa Lo prison in Hanoi. That shift may have been triggered by peace nego- tiations and a larger effort by the prison administration to centralize the captives in preparation for the end of the war and their release. An unintended consequence of these moves, from the Vietnamese perspective, was that it brought more of the POWs under the more direct influence of the SROs who were plotting a post-release public relations campaign in which their tough-guy never-say-die personas would be featured in the prisoners-at-war narrative—the story line they now forced on their underlings as theirs as well. According to Howes, prisoners arriving from the outlying camps were fed a virtual curriculum about the bad old days during which *all* Hoa Lo prisoners had been tortured before saying what their guards wanted to hear. This became the hero-prisoner story recounted to the press and to Hubbell, which he turned into his book *P.O.W.*

Another consequence, unforeseen by the SROs, was that the unruly voices coming in from the South harmonized with dissenting voices among the pilots that were not swallowing the SRO party line. There were subtle indications throughout the years that some pilots had second thoughts about the morality of the war they were fighting and skepticism about the prisoner-at-war theatrics they had been caught up in.[38] To begin with, there were the widely acknowledged statements against the war made by even the hardest of the hardcore SROs that were then justified—or explained away—as having been coerced. And there were pilot interviews with the peace travelers that revealed misgivings about the war. Air Force Captain Larry Carrigan, for example, told the October 1967 peace group that included Tom Hayden and Vivian Rothstein that reading Felix Greene's book *Vietnam! Vietnam!* had "kinda changed my mind" about the war. Tellingly, he then asked that they not quote him on that because "they've got prisons in the States also."[39]

By the time of the POWs' release and repatriation in early 1973, the war within the walls of Hoa Lo was more than that between prisoners and their guards. The tensions between officers and enlisted men, universal in military organizations, had hardened into class lines across which officers risked the welfare of enlisted men for the sake of their own hero-captive reputations and enlisted men openly dismissed the authority of the officers. Finally, to complicate matters, the solidarity of the SROs on which the prisoner-at-war narrative rested was shaken when two of the more senior-ranking officers, Edison Miller and Gene Wilber, added their voices to the cause of peace and rebuked the chain of command that Stockdale, Risner, and Denton had contrived.

By the time the POWs landed stateside, the press was as interested in the story of dissent within the prison population as anything else. The Pentagon and the Nixon White House, on the other hand, wanted

a different story told. Subsequent chapters in this book will recon-
struct how those competing narratives played out in the media and
political and popular culture.

2

Profiles of Dissent: Senior Officers

For his 1996 book, *The Wars We Took to Vietnam,* English professor Milton Bates studied the ways in which longstanding social conflicts within the United States played out in the war in Vietnam. Along with what he called the race, sex, and generation wars, he said that class wars rooted in domestic, occupational, and workplace social relations extended into the realities of in-country military life. "What the working-class conscripts found when they arrived in Vietnam," he wrote, "was—work."

War, Bates continued, has been compared with work, and work to war, pointing to Karl Marx's description of laborers as "privates of the industrial army . . . under the command of a perfect hierarchy of officers and sergeants." And just as workers resent the owners and managers who profit from their labor, "the worker-soldier had reason to resent those who were using him, the war's foremen and managers." Had Bates looked for evidence of the class war waged within the POW population, he would have found it there too, between senior officers and enlisted men and, unexpectedly, among the officers themselves.

LABORERS?—NOT IN THIS CLASS

POWs Edison Miller and Gene Wilber were uncharacteristic of the senior officer class. At ages thirty-six (Miller) and thirty-eight (Wilber) at time of capture, the two were among the most senior in years of service and age. They were career officers, Miller with more than eighteen years of service and Wilber with more than twenty years. They had previous combat experience, too, unlike many of the other captives: Wilber and Miller had completed air combat tours over Korea in the early 1950s. Miller flew the F-4U Corsair in support of Marine and Army ground troops and later served as a forward air controller, while Wilber flew the AD (later A-1) Skyraider on night strike missions from aircraft carriers, often landing in pitch darkness. They were combat-seasoned senior officers who had achieved fighter-squadron commanding officer roles. But their roots were lower class: they entered the military directly from high school and bypassed the normal college education prerequisite to become commissioned officers as aviators.

Despite their combat experience and advanced careers, they had developed and taken controversial stances against the war. Moreover, they were vocal and persistent in their dissent, using their rank, maturity, confidence in their experience, and perhaps even class background to disagree with the other SROs. These behaviors resulted in "stripping of rank" by the internal POW "chain of command" that the SROs claimed. Miller and Wilber were to be ignored, or worse, ostracized and shunned.

That Miller and Wilber differed from the other officers in the prisoner population by their persistent dissent coupled with their refusals to "accept amnesty"—as if the SROs had legal authority to offer it—by recanting and ceasing their dissenting actions is clearly established. It is less clear why they distinguished themselves the way they did, although social theory suggests that their upbringing, economic status, education level, and career paths, and in the case of Wilber, professed religious beliefs, set them apart from the "heroes" of the official story.

EDISON MILLER

Edison Miller was born Edward Grant Kennedy to a single mother in western Iowa on July 6, 1931. Days after his birth, she signed him over to an orphanage in Davenport in eastern Iowa. Miller describes being aware at a young age that he would have to market himself as a means to eventually get adopted, so he developed a sense of confidence and manner to win others over. The orphanage raised Edward Kennedy until Margaret Miller, a single woman attorney from Clinton, Iowa, adopted him at the age of five. With the means to support her compassion, Ms. Miller fostered and adopted ten children.

Ms. Miller gave five-year-old Edward a new name—Edison Wainwright Miller. She also gave him a role to model, as she was Miller's inspiration to become a lawyer, an occupation he practiced for nearly forty years after retiring from the military in 1973.

Miller speaks freely of his orphan years and his upbringing with a collection of adoptive siblings as having been an arena for learning to survive by communicating and promoting his own interests. As an orphan, he developed a confident extroversion as a means to secure an adopter. In a family setting after adoption, he learned to talk his way out of situations by convincing others of his viewpoint.

In his teens, Miller worked farm jobs and sold newspapers. In both work settings and school, he learned that he could enlist the help of others to get what he wanted by enticing them with food treats, typically doughnuts. Graduating from high school in Davenport, just shy of his eighteenth birthday, he enlisted in the Navy and began boot camp in July 1949. He tested highly across an array of exams and scored an IQ of 149.[1] Within his first ten months in the Navy, Seaman Miller was selected for the Naval Aviation Cadet (NAVCAD) program.

The skills that got Miller out of an orphanage and through his school years fast-tracked his Navy career. At flight school, he hung out with the schedulers, winning them over with doughnuts, coffee, and potato chips, and aligning himself with some of the Marine Corps flight instructors, who took a liking to his moxie and enthusiasm. Miller graduated ahead of his peers and, based on the urging of his flight instructors, opted for a commission as a second lieutenant in the Marine Corps, rather than an ensign rank in the Navy.

As a product of the NAVCAD program, Miller was part of a small minority in a population of college-educated aviation officers from the Naval Academy, ROTC, or Officer Candidate Schools. And having started flight training in his late teens, at age twenty he was two years younger than typical newly commissioned second lieutenants who graduated from college or the academies. In some ways, the NAVCAD path to aviator status is akin to the path to citizenship for an immigrant pursuing the American Dream: a path to great rewards potholed with the resentments of others who were humping the more "regular" paths. In casual settings such as the officers' clubs, it was not uncommon for officers to play out a kind of "caste order" of commissioning, with service academies such as Annapolis or West Point at the top, then ROTC and OCS/OTS programs, with the NAVCADs like Miller, with no college credentials, at the bottom. It was an informal pecking order with him at the low end. But it would not restrain the headstrong Miller.

Years later, he says he "did a lot of unconventional things" in his career: always willing to ask hard questions and never afraid to "challenge the system." He described himself as an iconoclastic rulebreaker: "Just tell Ed Miller the name of the game and he'll find the rules and beat you."[2]

Miller advanced in rank, gaining command of a fighter squadron that deployed to Chu Lai, South Vietnam, on July 5, 1967. From there they provided air support for ground operations below the DMZ and struck targets north of the DMZ. On October 13, 1967, north of Quang Tri Province, Miller and his radar intercept officer were hit. In a matter of seconds their plane was uncontrollable, and both ejected over hostile territory. Severely injuring several vertebrae during the ejection and breaking his ankle on parachute landing, Miller would spend more than forty days being held in field conditions before arriving in the prison facility at Hoa Lo in Hanoi.

After periods of initial interrogation and living in a cell by himself for a few weeks, Miller spent 1969 with other prisoners in Hoa Lo, and then to another detention facility, where he was joined by Gene Wilber when Wilber was moved from Hoa Lo in April 1970.

GENE WILBER

Edison Miller and Gene Wilber shared similarities in challenging upbringings and general career paths. They were from rural, farm, and working-class backgrounds and found employment and career paths in the military. In the detention system in Hanoi, the life experiences of Miller and Wilber were now set to converge.

Walter Eugene Wilber was born at home in rural north central Pennsylvania on January 17, 1930. His parents were tenant farmers, also known as sharecroppers. They worked for a landowner dairy farmer performing daily chores, milking, farm maintenance, planting, cultivating, and harvesting. This labor was in exchange for housing, produce, and a share of the profits, contingent upon the honesty of the landowner. It was a hard life; by the time Wilber was five, he could drive a team of horses. Once, helping load hay into the barn, he saw the trip-rope for the hay-carrier mechanism caught on his hayrack. With his dad beneath the load of hay, Wilber freed the rope, saving his dad from being crushed by hay. Wilber's hands bled from the rope burns so his mother slathered them with butter, wrapped them with flour sacks, and sent him out to get the cows home for milking—all in a day's work for a farmboy.

In 1942, with the Second World War underway, Wilber's parents took jobs in a factory, and were eventually able to buy a home. In the meantime, Wilber continued to work at farms. As early as age twelve, he was hired out to farmers during the summer months and received visits from his parents and siblings on Sundays. Sundays were important for Wilber, who received his "Christian education" at rural Baptist or Methodist churches, making a "decision for Christ" at thirteen. He would remain religious throughout his life, expressing protestant Christian beliefs through his identification and actions.

Wilber got a driver's license at sixteen, purchased a truck, and began driving a milk pickup route to local dairy farms, starting very early each morning and arriving at school late after delivering his truckload to the dairy plant. He maintained his studies, played basketball on the high school team, and graduated in 1947, in Troy,

Pennsylvania, four miles from the tenant farmhouse in which he had been born.

In the winter after his high school graduation, and sensing the Cold War mood enveloping the nation, Wilber enlisted in order to be a step ahead of the draft that he feared might dictate his choices. He had always wanted to learn to fly, so he enlisted in the Navy in 1948. After boot camp, schooling as an aviation electrician's mate, and getting some fleet experience, he entered the Naval Aviation Cadet (NAVCAD) program, just as Edison Miller would do the following year.[3]

Returning from deployments to Korea,[4] he continued through a progression of Navy jobs—flight instructor, flight deck officer on a carrier, jet fighter squadron pilot, and more. As a student in the ten-month graduate level program at Army Command and General Staff College, he excelled academically (his thesis graded as "superior") as the only non-college degreed officer in his class.

After a tour at Naval Air Force Atlantic Fleet as an operations officer on the admiral's staff, the young commander (thirty-five years old) had completed his professional grooming for the command pipeline. He next trained on F-4 Phantom IIs and joined Fighter Squadron 102 onboard USS *America* in early 1967 as executive officer, taking command of VF-102 on March 29, 1968, with orders to deploy the squadron with Carrier Air Wing Six to the Gulf of Tonkin.

During that period, Wilber was becoming more aware of controversies regarding conflict in Vietnam. In 1967, television news programs and the print media were reporting on protests, college unrest, and the October March on the Pentagon. At the same time, there was a reshuffling of Washington leadership surrounding the war in Vietnam that was leaving things unsettled. On November 1, 1967, Secretary of Defense Robert McNamara submitted a memorandum to President Johnson recommending de-escalation, stopping the bombing and turning over military responsibilities to the Republic of Vietnam. On November 29, McNamara submitted his resignation,[5] leaving his post on February 29, 1968. Amid that transition, Wilber was given command of a squadron with orders to go into combat. Two days later, on March 31, 1968, the commander-in-chief, President Johnson, announced abrupt changes in the war policy and "quit," announcing publicly that he would not seek reelection. The command structure far above Wilber's head had been reshuffled. On Monday morning, Wilber continued preparations for squadron deployment, and on April 10, 1968, they were underway for the western Pacific.

In the daily briefings from the Task Force Commander's staff, Wilber was confronted with rules of engagement that he annotated in his notebook as "confusing" along with reports from other pilots of operational command and control mistakes as war planners constantly adjusted to changing directions from the White House. On his twenty-first mission, on June 16, 1968, Wilber was shot down and found himself on the bank of a rice paddy west of Vinh, halfway between the DMZ and Hanoi, due to the mistaken decision of an air war commander miles away at sea.[6]

Having twisted his ankle on impact after a five-second parachute ride, Wilber was soon captured. Barefoot and blindfolded, he was led away, a young boy holding his hand and guiding him along a path. Wilber would not be heard from again for a year and a half, making an antiwar statement broadcast on Radio Hanoi in November 1969, the first confirmation for his family that he had been captured and was alive.

At the end of a nine-day trip by foot and truck from Vinh to Hanoi, Wilber suffered a stroke. Years later, the other POWs critical of his antiwar views would explain away the sincerity of his dissent by attributing it to a mix of stroke symptoms, trauma from the shootdown, and guilt for having lost his radar intercept officer—the PTSD-like explanation that later stigmatized the protests of other antiwar veterans as a mental health issue.

It's likely, however, that the stroke itself was brought on by logistical circumstances. The carrier had taken on bad water some weeks before, leaving Wilber and many shipmates weakened by dysentery. This had him dehydrated on the day he was shot down, and he was not given much to drink on the steaming-hot trip to Hanoi. Beckoned from the back of the truck at the entrance to Hoa Lo prison, Wilber could not stand. Carried inside, he could only sit on a stool if they propped it in a corner.

MILLER AND WILBER IN HANOI PRISONS

Miller was in Hoa Lo prison when Wilber arrived in late June of 1968, but they would not meet until April 1970. Wilber's first twenty-one months were spent living alone without contact with other Americans at Hoa Lo. The POW literature has used the term solitary confinement,[7] which might sound more ominous than it was. Some, but not all, new shootdowns were put in solitary, and Ralph Gaither, in his memoir *With God in a POW Camp*, said no one understood why.[8] Prison camp officials have said the reason was due to space. When there were more rooms than prisoners, nearly all were given single rooms, that is, put in solitary; as populations increased, prisoners were given roommates. Heard by Americans, solitary confinement connotes dungeon-like conditions, perhaps even a torture chamber—and that's the way Hubbell and Rochester and Kiley leave it. When pressed on it in a later interview, Wilber said his incarceration was "not very kind treatment" but that he "was not physically beaten or—or handled in this way, which we've heard described before."[9]

Released from solitary in April 1970, Wilber was moved from Hoa Lo to the facility the prisoners called the Zoo. About four kilometers southwest of Hoa Lo, the Zoo was originally a French film studio, Pha Phim.[10]

At the Zoo, Wilber would meet his first roommates, Miller and Commander Bob Schweitzer. Like Miller and Wilber, Schweitzer was a NAVCAD, having passed on college as an enlisted trainee, earning his officer's commission when he earned his aviator's wings.

Miller and Schweitzer had been exchanging views critical of the war before Wilber arrived. They were already somewhat notorious among the other pilots for a tape recording that had been played over the camps' public address systems; the other inmates derisively referred to the broadcast as "The Bob and Ed Show."

Bob: I think you're right, Ed. We have no business being in this war. It is strictly an affair for the Vietnamese to settle among themselves.

Ed: Not only do we have no business being here, our interference is illegal. It's an undeclared war of aggression, Bob, and that makes it downright criminal. That makes us criminals.

Bob: Actually, the Vietnamese government has every right to try us as war criminals. We have forfeited any rights under the Geneva Convention on the treatment of POWs. Ed, even the Code of Conduct has no application here.[11]

In their room at the Zoo, Wilber joined Miller and Schweitzer in discussions, sharing his thoughts about the impropriety of the war that he had come to realize during his time in solitary. On occasions, the three of them met together with visiting international delegations, but their most important exercise of dissent was through Canadian television journalist Michael Maclear.

THE MACLEAR TELEVISION INTERVIEW

Maclear was the only Western television journalist allowed into the Democratic Republic of Vietnam during the American war with Vietnam. He had reported on the funeral of Ho Chi Minh in September 1969, bringing news footage to American televisions. On his next trip, in December 1970, Maclear was taken to the Zoo on Christmas morning. He shot silent footage of the facilities, showing pilots Paul Brown, Mark Gartley, Edison Miller, Roger Ingvalson, Gene Wilber, Bob Schweitzer, and William Mayhew in the foreground. Maclear filmed a twenty-minute interview with Schweitzer and Wilber. Maclear's questions had been submitted to Wilber and Schweitzer ahead of time, and some of their responses had been approved by prison staff.

Maclear's film was developed in Tokyo and transmitted by satellite for an evening-news special on NBC and CBS on December 27. The CBS broadcast was introduced by Charles Collingwood, a network regular at the time. Acceding to the Cold War climate, Collingwood signaled to viewers that what they were about to see and hear was a Communist propaganda stunt in which U.S. prisoners of war were being used as props. The "plight" of the prisoners had become an issue in the negotiations to end the war, he said, and warned that the North Vietnamese authorities in Hanoi "were anxious to put their contention [*sic*] that all American prisoners of war in North Vietnam are well treated." What they were about to see, Collingwood advised, was "a carefully controlled Christmas interview with carefully selected American prisoners."[12]

Maclear then narrates what viewers are seeing as his camera pans across the camp and prisoners' living quarters:

The rooms, despite bars and bolts, could hardly be called cells.

Twenty feet wide by twelve, each had three beds but only two to a room were made up, two blankets on each.

Family pictures adorned and warmed some rooms.

Books were generally evident, and some newly arrived gum and gifts. But there are not many normal everyday articles, like ashtrays, pencil and paper or items of clothing.

Then the interview begins with Wilber and Schweitzer introducing themselves. With a Christmas tree in the background, they spoke without notes and did not appear to have been rehearsed. The format of the interview was straightforward, with brief to-the-point answers to each question. Maclear began with questions about the camp:

Maclear: Wilber and Schweitzer spoke easily, articulately, and with no trace of embarrassment. Some comments of no apparent significance were later censored.

What letters and parcels do you regularly receive, what do the parcels contain in them from your people, and what letters do you send?

Wilber: We get letters about every month, regularly about once a month, packages about every two months, and my packages usually contain candy and various food items, that uh, special little snacks, you know like peanuts and things like that, and sometimes some underwear, and small items. Chocolate candy and things we appreciate all the time, chewing gum.

Schweitzer: And, of course, our wives send the usual underwear, handkerchiefs, socks. We don't really need any clothing, but you know how wives are.

Maclear: And what mail do you send?

Schweitzer: We regularly send one letter a month. It's a regular form letter that both our families use and we use. It's been arranged by the Committee for Liaison, I believe, and the Vietnamese American Friendship Association. And I believe they go through Moscow. Through the new mail service, I believe from Moscow to New York and so on.

Wilber: Also, we occasionally send long letters for Christmas, Mother's Day, special occasions . . . we make radio messages for our children's birthdays, and our parents' birthdays, and our wives' birthdays. So we make many radio messages each year, many.[13]

For about a minute, Wilber and Schweitzer provide other details about the conditions such as meals, the books and magazines they had been given, and describe the events in Hanoi that they have been allowed to attend such as a Russian film production of Shakespeare's *Twelfth Night*, after which they were given an English edition of *The Complete Works of Shakespeare*. Then the interview turns more political:

Maclear: I want to ask do you talk to each other about war, what are your feelings on this, and what might you want to say directly to the American people?

Wilber: Yes, we discuss the war very much because the war is very close to us here. And we are all involved with it.

Schweitzer: I know I've had the deepest discussions I've ever had in my life with my fellow prisoners here. And we've had to go to the very core of our feelings on a number of things—loyalty, what is it, where does it lie; and morality, legality, a number of things that in our affluent, rushed life, I suppose in our country we don't normally give too deep thought about. But here we definitely do. I feel all of us do. And we've talked about it at great length, and how we feel.

Wilber: I think the answer of course is that the war must be ended, and it must be stopped now. We've just got to stop this thing. We've got to admit the facts as they lie and stop the war, and of course we must withdraw our troops to stop the war. That's a condition we have to face. So, once we do that the Vietnamese can solve their own problems, I'm confident of that. If we'll stop the war and get our troops out, that's what we have to do, and that's what the big job is.

Schweitzer: I of course agree, and, as I say, I'm terribly concerned about my country and I feel that the future of our country as well as Vietnam and Indochina cannot be served by the prolongation of this war, whatever the reasons and causes. I don't feel that it's necessary even to rake over the old reasons of who was wrong, who was right. It has been proven as far as I'm concerned. This war is bad, is bad, and it isn't going to improve, either our situation or the Vietnamese or Indochinese peoples' situation, they've got to be left alone.

Maclear: I want to thank you both. I think what you've had to say can only but help.

Collingwood then provided a summation for the program that avoided the message sent by Wilber and Schweitzer—that U.S. government and press claims of their mistreatment and subjection to mind control was anti-communist propaganda—and attacked the messengers. "Obviously," he said, "the North Vietnamese would not bring forward either recalcitrant or physically debilitated prisoners to be interviewed." The films and books that Wilber and Schweitzer had access to had "been restricted to propaganda and antiwar books, as is perhaps natural except for the works of Shakespeare which presumably are sanitized by now. . . . We can only hope all the other Americans prisoners of war in Vietnam had also been as well treated as those we have heard. That is obviously what the North Vietnamese want us to think."

Broadcast by NBC and CBS as a special report, at a time when American had only three network choices for television news and entertainment, ABC being the third, Maclear's report, with Collingwood's spin, could hardly have reached a wider audience. Attention to it was then amplified in the news cycle that followed, which continued to discount the message of Schweitzer and Wilber. The December 29 *New York Times* headlined, "Laird Discounts P.O.W. Interviews," referring to Melvin Laird, the secretary of defense, while the *Times*'s special correspondent, Christopher Lydon, reported on December 28 that a Pentagon spokesman declared the camp shown by Maclear to be a "showplace."[14] White House press secretary Ron Ziegler quoted President Nixon's comment that the North Vietnamese facilitation of the interview was a "total disregard of the terms and intentions of the Geneva Conventions."

AFTER MACLEAR

The thumbs-down press response to the Wilber and Schweitzer testimonies might have discouraged the POW dissenters. After all, if the public could not be rallied to the courage of their heartfelt pleas for peace, what chance was there that the war could be ended, and that they would be spared social and legal reproach upon return, if and when that came to pass? Nevertheless, the rebel captives stayed the course, producing, in Hubbell's words, "all kinds of the most virulent antiwar even anti-American, material for the enemy." As an example, Hubbell quoted Ed Miller's 1971 Mother's Day message:

> Today, America's mothers must face the fact that their sons are killing fellow human beings and destroying foreign countries for

an unjust cause, making our actions not only illegal, but immoral.
... My personal participation in this war is my personal shame
and tragedy. My country's immoral and illegal actions which are
now culminated in the tragedy of Vietnam is America's shame.[15]

According to Hubbell, on July 4 Miller and Wilber tape-recorded
an open letter to the American people in which they described themselves as patriotic officers dedicated to their country who had been
deceived by their leaders into committing acts against Indochina that
were immoral and barbaric. They ended with an Independence Day
wish for the success of the antiwar movement.

Changes were afoot, however. At the same time Maclear was in
Hanoi, the Vietnamese were closing smaller camps such as the Zoo
and consolidating prisoners into the Hanoi city-center prison, Hoa
Lo. The move was prompted by the U.S. special forces raid on the
Son Tay camp just outside Hanoi the previous November, and by the
prison authorities' desire to manage more closely the prison population as negotiations to end the war proceeded.

Meanwhile, the Defense Department and press reaction to the
Maclear interview had prefigured a Pentagon counterstrike against
POW dissent in Hanoi. Coincidentally, the crackdown was simplified
with Wilber, Miller, and their sympathizers now consolidated under
the thumb of the hardline SROs in Hoa Lo. In midsummer 1971, the
Navy's James Stockdale ordered Wilber, Miller, and Schweitzer to
"Write Nothing for the V. Meet no delegations. Make no tapes. No
early releases."[16] He finished by demanding to know from them: "Are
you with us?"

Schweitzer responded to Stockdale's order equivocally, saying
"each man should make his own decision" but that he was "in general agreement with Commander Stockdale."[17] In August, he agreed
to amnesty from prosecution that was threatened by the SROs and
rejoined the SRO-designed prisoner command structure. In return,
he agreed not to make any more statements nor participate in any
more interviews.

Wilber and Miller responded forthrightly: "We actively oppose this war." Wilber's commitment to peace was a "matter of conscience" supported by his deeply held religious beliefs. He had concluded while in solitary confinement that the war was not declared legally, and that an order forbidding him to express his opinion was not a "lawful" order under the Uniform Code of Military Justice.[18] He believed that his First Amendment rights as a citizen prevailed, and that the dynamic nature of the military required a robust discussion in order to get to the best decisions.

On August 11, after being offered amnesty in exchange for their refusal to desist from public objections to the war—the offer that Schweitzer had accepted—Robinson Risner advised Wilber and Miller, "You are hereby relieved of your military authority."[19]

In their last year of captivity, Miller and Wilber gave more interviews and made several more statements. In May 1972, with six other POWs, they spoke with a team of peace activists that included Clergy and Laity Concerned's Reverend Robert Lecky, Catholic priest Father Paul Meyer, president of the National Student Association Margery Tabankin, and Bill Zimmerman representing Medical Aid to Indochina; in July along with five other POWs they met with actress and activist Jane Fonda, and in August with former U.S. attorney general Ramsey Clark.[20]

The so-called Christmas Bombings of 1972 resulted in ninety-two American fliers being shot down (thirty-three KIA, thirty-three POW, twenty-six rescued); the prison population swelled with thirty-three more captured pilots being brought into Hoa Lo. Many of the new captives were young junior officers who were warned through the prisoner grapevine to steer clear of Miller and Wilber, as new captives had been warned for some years by then. Years later, however, one of the newer shootdowns remembered there having been something compelling about these two senior officers who defied convention and knowingly risked their careers despite threats of legal punishment.[21]

Together with Wilber and Miller, six of the newbies shot down in 1971 and early 1972 signed letters decrying the "many innocent people dying a totally needless and senseless death" in the bombings.

The letters were addressed to senators and representatives and media leaders, including newscaster Walter Cronkite.[22]

RELEASE, RETURN, REJECTION

Threats by SROs to punish the pilots who had spoken out against the war, and the anxiety of the dissident pilots about trials, ruined careers, and prison time, were put in abeyance by Secretary of Defense Melvin Laird's declaration that alleged offenses by POWs were to be forgiven.[23]

Had Wilber and Miller gone to trial, it is likely their defenses would have taken very different forms. Miller, characterized by his fellow prisoners as "a lawyer," would argue there was insufficient evidence to support the charges. Wilber, on the other hand, didn't deny the substance of the charge that he had made statements opposing the war, but he remained convinced that the war was wrong and that his objections to it were morally justified. In late March, Wilber was contacted by Mike Wallace for an interview on the CBS *60 Minutes* show that was filmed on April 1 and aired the same evening. If Wilber had thought Wallace would reprise Maclear's straightforward questions about the conditions of his imprisonment, he would be surprised. Wallace set up Wilber for a "brainwash" indictment in his opening monologue:[24]

Tonight, a POW, a Navy captain who says he was not tortured in Hanoi, a man who made antiwar statements broadcast by Radio Hanoi. . . . Wilber says he made his antiwar statements in Hanoi voluntarily. More on that story from Captain Wilber when *60 Minutes* continues.

Not so subtly, Wallace was cueing his viewers that Wilber had not sought relief from physical pain by making the statements against the war, an explanation that all Americans could understand and sympathize with, but that he had fallen prey to communist mind-control tactics. He had been *persuaded* to make his statements, not *coerced*.

Without ever actually alleging that Wilber had been programmed to renounce his loyalty to America, Wallace had cleverly trapped the captain in a kind of damned-if-you-do, damned-if-you-don't conundrum: Wilber could either contradict his previous statements about not having been tortured—and thereby destroy his own credibility and demonize the Vietnamese—or he could deny, as Miller was doing, that he had made the statements at all.

Wallace seemed most intent on forcing Wilber to denounce the Vietnamese for torture and, failing that, impugn Wilber's character.

Wallace: Captain Wilber, we've heard so many awful tales of torture of our POWs this week, all week long. What was your experience?

Wilber: Well, I was not tortured.

Wallace: Surely you have no reason to disbelieve the stories that we're hearing, then, from your fellow officers.

Wilber: No, sir, I would not disbelieve them or attempt to repudiate them in any way. It's something that each person has to tell his own story.

Wallace: Someplace along the line in prison camp—maybe it was while you were in solitary—you apparently changed your mind about the war. After all, you were a career officer—you weren't a child. You were already in your late thirties.

Wilber: Uh-huh.

Wallace: What changed your mind about the war? What made you—

Wilber: Well, I think, my conscience. I happen to be a Christian and found out that my conscience bothered me. And so, the—the big old bugaboo that we hear—conscience and morality—started to show itself. We have to look at things in, in the total picture of legality and morality. And as I had time to sit for many hours . . . I had time to really find out what Gene Wilber was like.

Wallace: When your fellow POWs learned that you were making antiwar statements—and you did, more than once—meeting with American antiwar groups in Hanoi, and so forth, what was their reaction to you?

Wilber: Well, it was varied, and this is not unusual. Some concurred,

some encouraged it, some said, "I'm with you, but don't include
me." There—it was just a whole range of feelings. . . .

Wallace: Well—do you know Captain James Mulligan?

Wilber: I know him very briefly.

Wallace: The reason I ask is that he, another naval officer, another
POW, is quoted in the *New York Times* just this morning as
saying, "No one ever minds anyone breaking under torture. But
it's those guys who fink out who get you. Those guys will get
what's coming to them."

Moments later, Wallace returned to Mulligan's threat that Wilber and
other dissidents "will get what's coming to them." Some of those guys,
Wallace repeated, "They say that they're—they're going to get you. They
say they're going to—they're going to follow this through. There's talk
of court-martial, there's talk of ostracism." Wallace had gone out of his
way to quote Mulligan's words from the *Times* story, and his reiteration
of "get you" hung in the air as the interview ended. Had he gotten wind
of plans for violence against Wilber, Miller, and others? By alluding to
its possibility, had he, if inadvertently, encouraged just that?

Howes in fact wrote in *Voices of the Vietnam POWs* that one SRO
in April 1972 had issued a "conditional license to kill" fellow POWs if
their loyalty to the United States was suspect. The circumstances surrounding the threat will be clarified in chapter 5 of this book, but the
likelihood that Wallace was privy to the story, otherwise unreported,
raises questions about who leaked it to him and for what purpose
other than to unnerve Wilber and provoke real harm to him and the
other dissidents.

The prescience of Wallace's allusion to violence was soon dem-
onstrated. On May 24, President Nixon hosted the POWs, spouses,
and dates for a White House reception. It was a gala affair with more
than 500 former POWs in service dress uniforms with spouses and
dates in evening dress. Earlier in the afternoon, after a briefing of
Navy former POWs with the CNO, Admiral Zumwalt, Wilber and
his wife returned to their hotel to prepare for the evening dinner
events, only to find out that their room had been broken into. The

word "TRAITOR!" was written in lipstick across the mirror, among a few other epithets; a fishbowl with goldfish had been placed in the room (evoking the trope that antiwar POWs had an aquarium as a part of alleged special treatment by their captors); and personal items were in disarray.

The Wilber hotel room break-in was the kind of calling-card operation that sent the message: "We can get you when we want." In the paranoid climate surrounding the Watergate break-in that was bringing down the Nixon presidency, it was not an uncommon tactic. But Wilber did not report the incident, and it proved to be a one-off event.

The threat of courts-martial and ostracism, also alluded to by Wallace, were more fully realized. When Secretary of Defense Laird declined to bring Defense Department charges against the dissidents, he left open the possibility that *individual* POWs were free to file charges against other individuals, and that's what Rear Admiral James Stockdale did. In late June 1973, he charged Wilber and Miller with "mutiny, aiding the enemy, conspiracy, soliciting other prisoners to violate the Code of Conduct, and causing or attempting to cause insubordination and disloyalty."[25]

A three-month investigation by Navy Secretary John W. Warner dismissed the charges, saying courts-martial would be disruptive to those who would have to testify. In September 1973 he issued letters of censure to Wilber and Miller, charging them with failing to meet the standards expected of officers of the armed forces and announced they would be retired in "the best interests of the naval service."[26]

The ostracism foreseen in the Wallace interview also loomed. Ad hominem humiliations such as Wallace's infantilizing remark that Wilber was "not a child" would dovetail with the SROs' attempt to distinguish their upright manliness as hardcore loyalists from the weaklings who had sought relief from torture in return for giving aid and comfort to the enemy. The projection of weakness onto fellow prisoners like Wilber and Miller, who were less educated and less privileged by class background, would be most apparent in the attitude shown by SROs toward enlisted men who returned with them—the subject of the next chapter.

Ostracizing of that type was ingrained in the notion of brainwashing that was carried from the post–Korean War studies of POW defection into the years of the war in Vietnam. The psychologizing of dissent characteristic of those studies became, in turn, the backstory to the medicalizing of GI, veteran, and POW rejection of war, discussed in subsequent chapters.

3

Profiles of Dissent: "The Peace Committee" of Enlisted POWs

*The enlisted status of those in the Peace Committee made
damning them relatively easy.*

—CRAIG HOWES

The media spotlight on the pilots returning from Hanoi in 1973 overshadowed the news about returning ground troops.[1] News organizations were far more interested in a few pilots like Ed Miller and Gene Wilber accused of collaboration than in the men captured in the South and eventually moved to the Hanoi prison facilities. Most of the latter group were Marines and Army soldiers. Few were officers. Among them were eight enlisted men known as the Peace Committee.[2]

Charges were brought against "The Eight" by Air Force Colonel Theodore Guy. While not from the same background of service academia as James Stockdale, who charged the dissident pilots, Guy's pedigree was nevertheless privileged in comparison with the men he accused. His father was a professional musician who had traveled with the Dorsey Brothers band. Guy had attended Kemper Military School in Missouri and then was wait-listed for admission to West

Point. Impatient and wanting to get his military career underway, he joined the Air Force in 1949. Over Korea, he won two Distinguished Flying Crosses and six Air Medals.[3]

Prior to his capture in Laos, Guy had also known a war in Vietnam that was far removed from that of the men he would accuse. The night before getting shot down, he had enjoyed a bucket of popcorn and a couple of drinks in his "sleeping trailer" after returning from another mission to his F-4 base at Cam Ranh Bay. In the morning, he had a breakfast of scrambled eggs and toast "at the club" before taking off and being shot down later in the day. Guy was captured on March 22, 1968. His back-seater did not survive the shootdown.[4]

On May 29, 1973, Colonel Guy charged the eight enlisted men with "aiding and abetting the enemy, accepting gratuities, and taking part in a conspiracy against the U.S. government." As characterized by the historians Stuart Rochester and Fredrick Kiley in their 1998 book *Honor Bound: American Prisoners of War in Southeast Asia, 1961–1973*, a reiteration of John Hubbell's *P.O.W.*, the men in Guy's crosshairs were:

> soldiers and Marines "captured in . . . South Vietnam . . . young enlistees, "grunts," average guys from ordinary backgrounds suddenly thrust into extraordinary circumstances [and] victimized as much by their youth and inexperience as by the South's peculiarly adverse conditions. The dozen or so . . . averaged barely 20 years of age, 12 years less than the aviator-officers incarcerated. . . . Their lack of training and PW organization inherent in the Southern situation, left them especially ill-equipped to deal with the psychological demands of captivity. . . . As a group they tended to be less stable and steadfast and coped less successfully than older, more seasoned hands.[5]

Drawn by Rochester and Kiley, this profile of the dissenting enlisted men was a composite of the captives' demographic details—their young ages, for example—and the authors' conformity to what had become, by the time they wrote in the 1990s, the prevailing condescension that enlisted men's own shortcomings had betrayed them. Had Rochester and Kiley drilled more deeply into the available material on The Eight, they might have found their dissent rooted in the same structure of class hierarchy as that of the antiwar pilots. James Daly's biography makes the point.

JAMES DALY

The strongest case that dissent was motivated by conscience is made by James Daly in his 1975 memoir written with Lee Bergman. Rochester and Kiley knew about the book and used it to document some details of camp life of the prisoners taken in the South, but nowhere in their *Honor Bound* did the authors use the memoir to profile Daly, the person.

Daly arrived in Chu Lai, South Vietnam, in October 1967 and was immediately moved, emotionally, by the despair of the Vietnamese. "I really felt sorry for [the kids]," he wrote, "skinny, torn shirts, bare feet, big sad eyes just staring at you." He also felt the Vietnamese "hatred for the Americans," based, he thought, "on the misery of [the] peasants and farmers [having] suffered through so many years of war."[6]

Assigned to Alpha Company of the 196th Light Infantry Brigade, Daly was wounded and captured by North Vietnamese soldiers after a fierce firefight on January 9, 1968, in the Que Son Valley west of Tam Ky. He was handed over to forces of the NLF and moved from camp to camp with other captives known later as the Kushner group.[7] Taken 500 miles by foot, truck, and train to Hanoi, the group arrived in April 1971 at a prison in Hanoi about a kilometer north of the Hoa Lo prison known by the Americans as Plantation.[8] There, they learned about the Peace Committee (PC), a group of POWs said to be sympathetic to the North Vietnamese; one of the prison guards showed the newcomers a magazine published by the PCs called *New Life*. The PCs, said the guard, "believe the war is wrong and are helping to bring it to an end."[9]

Daly's initial dissent took form in discussions with roommates about whether to write letters home expressing antiwar views. "As it turned out," he wrote in his memoir, "all the guys in the room agreed to write, and probably most everyone in the camp did, also." He addressed one letter to the American people and one to the mayor of New York City. In his letters, he "denounced the war and questioned why millions were being spent to bomb the Indochinese people, and how this money was needed at home."[10]

At Christmastime 1971, Daly and roommates were allowed to mingle for the first time with the PCs. By then, he was reflecting on the Vietnamese people he had met in the South, the troops heading south on the Trail, and the prison staff at Plantation. He thought about the history of Vietnam's struggle against European colonialism, which he had learned about reading the periodical *Vietnamese Studies*, Felix Greene's *The Enemy*, and *The Pentagon Papers*, all furnished by the guards. As he would recall later, "I knew in my gut *what I had believed before in my head*—that the war was wrong, and we had no right to be there tearing this country to pieces." When the PCs invited Daly to join them and move to their quarters, he accepted the offer.[11]

Daly's Vietnam experience might have precipitated his coming to conscience, but his words, italicized above, belie the singularity of his experience as the difference-maker in his turn against the war. Rather, it was the chemistry of his time at war and in captivity with his growing-up experience that was epiphanous.[12]

Daly was Black. He grew up as a Baptist in the Bedford-Stuyvesant section of Brooklyn. As a twelve-year-old, he hardly ever missed a Sunday church service. He really liked the church, especially "joining the different clubs and going on trips." In 1959, "a lady selling magazines" introduced the family to the Jehovah's Witness religion. His mother became a member. James did not because it involved a commitment to 100 hours a week as a Pioneer going door-to-door to spread the faith. He thought it more important to get a job to help his mother, who struggled to support seven kids. But he learned and understood the principles of the religion and subscribed to its teachings on war.[13]

Daly's father was strict and never played with him or encouraged him to take part in sports. His father left the family while James was still in school. Mostly, he wrote, he stayed in the house and helped with the cooking and cleaning. He took odd jobs "cleaning houses, washing windows or cars, and even baking cakes and pies on the holidays."[14] The jobs earned him only five dollars a week, but with that he could buy things his mother could not afford, like clothes, and still give some money to her.

Graduating from Franklin K. Lane High School in June 1966 with plans to attend community college, James took a job clerking at B. Altman's department store. However, U.S. involvement in Vietnam was deepening and he felt the draft breathing down his neck. Upon visiting an Army recruitment center, he was told, "As a conscientious objector you can pick the kind of noncombat job you want. After basic training, the choice is yours."[15]

Basic training was hard. With few physical skills, he was remanded to extra pushups. He thought the marching cadences like "Jody's got your girl and gone—Jody's got your mama, too" were insulting. But he kept his mouth shut. When he didn't yell "Kill!" on the bayonet course and explained to the sergeant that he didn't believe in killing, the sergeant called him a "pussy."[16] Through it all, James believed that a noncombat job awaited him at the end of basic training. After all, that's what the recruiter had promised. Upon completion of basic, however, he learned that the guarantee was good only for those who had enlisted for four years. James was a draftee with a two-year obligation, and was headed now to Fort Polk in Louisiana for advanced infantry training.

Daly's weeks at Fort Polk were filled with appointments, phone calls, and paper filings in pursuit of the conscientious objector status he desired. He had a "mental hygiene consultation" with a psychiatrist, meetings with two different chaplains and the commander of the 3rd Training Brigade, who suggested his best option: "Go home on leave—and stay home! Let the MPs pick you up. You'll be charged with AWOL, but you'll get attention and be able to plead your case."

At home on leave before shipment to Vietnam, Daly looked into flights to Sweden where draft resisters and deserters were finding sanctuary. He consulted the "head overseer" of his family's Jehovah's Witness congregation to see about an endorsement for his application for CO status. The overseer declined to help, upbraiding James for not accepting a Pioneer mission that would have credentialed his religious claim as a CO. Nor could the overseer countenance desertion: "You are in the service now and you must go by the rules and regulations of the military."[17]

Daly made one last appeal, appearing in person at Fort Hamilton in Brooklyn where he was told to wait until he arrived at Oakland Army Terminal in California where he would be processed for Vietnam—and to raise the issue there. In Oakland he was told again to wait, and to take up the matter with his new unit when he got to Vietnam.

Daly was in Vietnam only about three months before he was captured. From that point on, his biography as a dissident POW begins paralleling the lives of his newly made comrades-in-captivity. With remarkable sociological intuition, Daly seems to have sensed the class backgrounds common to PCs as a basis for mutuality and the strengthening of his own commitments to conscience. In the group of eight enlisted men eventually charged for misconduct, that affinity was felt first and most deeply with Bob Chenoweth.

BOB CHENOWETH

Daly did not meet Chenoweth until Christmas 1971 when the prisoner groups segregated at Plantation were freed to socialize together. Daly recognized him immediately as the leader of the Peace Committee. "There was never any question about his sincerity, involvement, or understanding of the PC goals."[18]

Chenoweth had joined the Army in 1966 and was trained to work on UH-1 Huey helicopters. He arrived in Vietnam in January 1967 and began flying combat, medevac, and resupply missions as a crew chief. On February 8, 1968, he was flying back to Da Nang in the beat-up Huey, with a black cat painted on its nose, when it came under heavy ground fire and crashed in a cemetery.[19] All six men on board got out, but they were quickly hemmed in by local NLF forces, and surrendered. Chenoweth was twenty and would spend the next five years in enemy hands.

Chenoweth had been in Vietnam for only a year. But like Daly, he had developed an empathy for the Vietnamese people and a distaste for the racist views of most Americans toward the Vietnamese. In a 2017 interview, Chenoweth reflected that he couldn't see how U.S. forces could possibly be helping the Vietnamese given the attitude that GIs had, viewing them as "subhuman" and disparaging them as "gooks and dinks."

Chenoweth was born in Portland, Oregon, December 31, 1947. His dad was a telephone company technician and a Second World War Navy vet, having served on submarines out of Hawaii. He remembers:

The family rented houses and apartments and lived from paycheck to paycheck. When we got a little older, we picked beans, berries and nuts at the local farms. We would get to keep a little money for a toy, but most went to Mom. I don't remember a time when I had my own bedroom. I did not mind or think it unusual since I had little to compare my life to anyone else.

I grew up believing America was the best place to live. I watched John Wayne and all the rest. I started building model airplanes when I was a little kid and still make models today. We played with neighbor kids including John whose family was Mexican and owned a Mexican Restaurant. John's mom was very sweet and fed us neighbor kids tacos. It was my first exposure to another culture.

Chenoweth grew up with racial sensitivities, his father being from the North and his mother from the South, with "that open outspoken self-assurance that whites were superior." In Portland he was "exposed to Black people, as well as Japanese and Chinese kids," enabling the development of his own sense of those he would befriend. At Portland's Benson Polytechnic School he was a drummer in the band and became best friends with Black kids, helping them to join the Drum and Bugle Corps to which he belonged. Chenoweth remembers a "great civics teacher in his senior year" who really helped him understand the civil rights struggle. But he says:

It was the Army experience in both Louisiana and Alabama that shocked me into the reality of race. I pulled a lot of KP in basic training and almost always did so with Black soldiers. We talked a lot since I was curious about their lives especially in the south. One guy I met had been a high school science teacher in Mississippi before being drafted. He said there was a Black HS and a white HS in his town. He talked about the differences in equipment, classes and textbooks. What he was telling me outraged me since it went against what I believed it was like to be Americans. . . . The poverty I witnessed was also a bit of a surprise. Just to see it. Again, I did not understand about "institutional racism," etc. but I remembered what I saw. I found Army training to be the foundation of the race hatred soldiers later exhibited toward the Vietnamese.

When Chenoweth got to his helicopter unit in Vietnam in January 1967 a Black crew chief became a mentor. He introduced Chenoweth to "Ti Ti Boy, a Vietnamese guy who bought cigarettes, soap, records and other PX items. Ti Ti Boy hated Nguyen Van Thieu, Nguyen Cao Ky, and all the rest of the 'General Presidents.' I also witnessed press gangs rounding up young men for the South Vietnamese Army (ARVN), often under great duress."

The contact that ground troops had with Vietnamese before they were captured distinguished them from the pilots who had had no, or little, exposure to Vietnam and its people prior to being shot down. And that difference continued into their prison experience. Chenoweth remembered the work crews he was assigned to at the Portholes camp in Nghe Anh Province:

[At the] the camp in Nghe An we went out of our rooms most days to repair bomb shelters, do garden work (planted watermelons, other melons, cassava, peanuts, greens, etc.), and to help in the rice fields. . . . We also went out sometimes in the early evening to go to another village and get supplies. We carried rice, blankets, giant woks, cooking tools, sugar, POW cloths etc.

which we would bring back to our camp and others. . . . When we went to get supplies, mostly people were kind to us and curious . . . the supplies were for us, the villagers and the guards, and our camp.

In Ha Tay Province our outdoor work was cleaning and gardening. We planted and tended to various plants including kohlrabi, bok choy, onions, and other greens. Once on a run, this French guy, Goiun, was carrying a huge wok. He had it over his back holding each handle in his hands. I was behind him [when] this old lady jumped out from behind a bush and wacked him with a bamboo stick. Goiun moaned and dropped. He dropped the wok and it made a thud. Duc [the village turnkey] ran up and got hold of her, pleading, "Grandmother, grandmother." Even at the time I thought it was one of the funniest things I had ever seen.

Chenoweth recalls "falling in" with King David Rayford Jr. and Alfonso Riate "just because of what I had experienced."

KING DAVID RAYFORD

Chenoweth recalled that the Peace Committee germinated with him, Rayford, and Riate while they were held at the Portholes prison camp in Nghe Anh province near the North Vietnamese city of Vinh. It was a relief for some prisoners to be there, better sheltered, fed, and treated for injuries than they had been in the jungle camps in the South.[20]

Rayford had been captured in July 1967 and was merged, en route, into the "Purcell bunch" that included Chenoweth, arriving at Portholes in April 1968.

Ray [Rayford] and I were next to each other at Portholes where he told me his background and upbringing. He was a 20-year-old African American drafted off the Ford assembly line in Detroit. He came from sharecroppers in Mississippi as I recall. His grandma sent him up to Chicago. Ray had worked, had a little boy, and been injured working on an upholstery machine at a company that made barber chairs. His hand was damaged, and he had two stiff fingers. I found it incredible that he had been drafted and accepted into the Army. Ray did too. He was one of the most honest and hardworking people I had ever met. When we went out to work [from the Portholes camp] we often got pieces of pineapple, or peanuts from the villagers.[21]

It was with Rayford, in the Portholes camp, that the Peace Committee began to take shape. They were soon joined in the effort by Riate.

ALFONSO RIATE

If the Damned Eight story was to be made into a film, the trailer for it would feature Alfonso Riate. Riate was born in Sebastopol, California. His dad was Filipino and died when Al was very young. His mom was Native American from the Karuk tribe. She was famous as a tribal elder and teacher of the tribe's language. Riate's granddad practiced Indian traditional medicine. Al and his younger brother John eventually moved to Los Angeles where they lived alone. Al forged papers so they could go to high school.[22]

Chenoweth remembered meeting Riate at Portholes:

I both admired and respected him right from the start. We got to that camp sometime in April 1968. The camp was a microcosm of life back home. When our group came [into Portholes], including Rayford, we quickly divided up along "race lines" (for lack of a better term). I had a long hatred for racist bullshit that went back to my high school days. Rayford and I talked about race, slavery, and the like since we were next to each other.

I can tell you that Al had a very hard early life, but I know it was not a life without love. Reservation life, and all its hardship and injustice and racism, is not widely understood by "white America," even today. In the 50s and 60s it was brutal. Al's decision to leave the reservation for LA with his brother showed both strength and courage.

After high school, Riate took classes at Long Beach Community College and joined the Marines in 1965. He volunteered for duty in Vietnam and went to K company, 3rd Battalion, 3rd Marine Division (K-3-3). He was captured while on an operation near Hill 861 in Quang Tri Province.

Al once tried to escape from Portholes. His Filipino-Indian ancestry gave him a dark complexion—and the best chance that any of us could be mistaken for a Vietnamese. He had also learned a little Vietnamese language. On a work detail out of the camp, he escaped. Two days later, he walked into an NVA anti-aircraft site, sat down for tea with the soldiers! One of [the NVA] went off shortly after that and after a while the camp guards came down the trail to take him back to camp.

Chenoweth's lesson from Riate's attempted getaway was "You can get out of the camp but not out of the country!"

In a screenwriter's hands, the character of a mixed-race Marine who walked onto an enemy firebase and sat for tea might get embellished as a writer, soldier-poet, and singer-songwriter. But Riate was all of those, too. While captive, he wrote a protest song in Vietnamese and later recorded it.[23]

In April 1972, U.S. B-52 bombers rolled in on Hanoi. In his memoir, Daly remembered feeling close to the Vietnamese. "All I could picture," he wrote, "was some man or woman or little kid being shattered to pieces by an American bomb."[24] During the raid, Daly remembered, Riate had started writing a letter to the prison administrator. When the bombing stopped, Daly and the others gathered around him to read what he had written. The letter acknowledged that the antiwar statements the PCs had been making up to that point were not enough to help end the war. Daly remembered the rest of the letter:

[Riate] wanted to do more than that, he was even ready to consider joining the North Vietnamese Army. . . . For a minute we all just stood there, thinking over Riate's words. Then Chenoweth and [John] Young asked Riate if they could sign the letter also.

"Well, that's up to you," Riate said. "I wrote it as being only from me since I didn't know if all the rest of you had the same feelings."

Then, one by one, each of us spoke out on how we felt the same and wanted to sign. My going along didn't come easily. My emotions were all for it—but it was like a double-edged knife. I think we all found it hard to believe we would even consider bearing arms against the United States.[25]

Colonel Guy, the self-appointed authority figure over the enlisted prisoners, announced the letter-signing to the prison population and threatened that the PCs could be "eliminated" or "liquidated" for their allegiance to Hanoi. The prison camp administration expressed its concern for the safety of The Eight from prisoner-on-prisoner violence through Major Do Xuan Oanh. Xuan Oanh spoke candidly with them about the open situation in Hoa Lo when prisoners were allowed to move about the facility with fewer restrictions after the Peace Accords were signed. The Eight were reassured by the awareness of the prison staff to watch out for them—and keep them safe from their fellow American prisoners.[26]

Riate's letter would later be the basis for Guy's charges against The Eight for "conspiracy against the U.S. government."[27]

JOHN YOUNG

From what we know, John Young did not come into the military with the sensitivities to race and class that Daly, Chenoweth, Rayford, and Riate did. He described himself as more middle class than the others and told Zalin Grant that he had not heard of Vietnam before coming to Fort Bragg for training. "Laos and Cambodia I knew were someplace in Asia, but I certainly could not have placed them on a blank map," he told Grant. "Nor was I familiar with the definition of communism." Young had also gone into the military unaware of the antiwar movement. "I assumed it was an isolated thing by hippies and radicals," he told Grant. His capture on January 31, 1968, was his wake-up call.

Young was an Army Specialist Green Beret captured while leading a patrol of Lao mercenaries near the Long Vei Special Forces (Green Beret) camp near the Demilitarized Zone. The camp would be overrun on February 7, handing the United States one of the most significant losses of the war. Badly wounded, he was carried by hammock for about a month along jungle trails until reaching a house belonging to the Bru minority of the Montagnard people. Young told Grant of the treatment he received from the Bru:

> They brought me breakfast and supper of soup and rice balls. I was given my own private basket of potatoes and manioc. Villagers returning from the fields always made sure the basket was full. . . . They were gentle farmers. And I began to reexamine my thoughts about the war . . . realized I knew little about Vietnam or why we were there.[28]
>
> Before this time, I couldn't have given anyone a definition of colonialism. . . . Neither could I define capitalism. I had my own definition, I guess: "The American Way of Life."[29]

By August 1968, Young had been moved to a camp at Duong Ke (called by prisoners Farnsworth, or D-1) about thirty kilometers south-southwest of Hanoi where a North Vietnamese guard gave him books to read, telling Young, "We want you to understand our side." Six of those books were authored by Americans, and Australian Wilfred Burchett's *Mekong Upstream* was particularly influential. "In the United States," he recalled, "I had heard of Southeast Asia in terms of 'the communists.' Now I was reading the human story of the people."

When Ho Chi Minh died on September 2, 1969, Young saw the

guards wearing black armbands and his chief jailer, Le Van Vuong, trying to hold back his tears. "But he couldn't," said Young. "He started crying. I cried too."[30] Four days later Young volunteered to make a tape to be sent home with a visiting group of U.S. peace activists. The tape expressed his support for the antiwar movement and "marked the beginning of my protest," he told Grant.[31]

Vuong was nicknamed "Cheese" by the prisoners because, as Young says they told him, "in America the man in charge is called the head cheese. He smiled broadly":

> We came to like him very much. It was just that he really believed so hard, so much, in what he was doing. And I think he tried to be as fair as he could with us. I learned to look at him as a friend. He was sort of like an uncle. He taught us patience and understanding.[32]

By contrast, Cheese, as portrayed by SROs in Hubbell's official story, was "full of hatred for his American prisoners [and] soon revealed himself to be a sadist." Hubbell continued unremittingly in that vein, describing heinous acts of torture such as Vuong reaching into Air Force Captain Edward Leonard Jr.'s eye sockets, "fasten[ing] his small fingers on the eyeballs and squeezing them and roll them for long agonizing minutes."[33]

Young remembered making thirty-three tapes for the North Vietnamese, and writing letters to President Nixon, to Congress, to GIs, and to people in his hometown. In letters to GIs, he explained the war and urged them to follow their own consciences.[34]

MICHAEL BRANCH AND FRED ELBERT

We don't have the background on Michael Branch and Fred Elbert that we have for the other enlisted POWs. Young described Branch as an "extremely poor country boy" who was an Army truck driver captured near Utah Beach in Quang Tri Province and "as much opposed to the war as I was."[35] Like the profiles of the other dissenting POWs,

Branch's class background distinguished him from the officers charging them.

Hubbell refers to a May 14, 1971, "memo signed by 'Michael P. Branch, deserter'" which read, "I've joined with a group of captured servicemen who are against the war in Vietnam." The memo advised GIs to "refuse combat or just botch up all your operations" and to "get in touch with the local people who will notify the Viet Cong [who] will get you to a liberated area [and] help you get to any country of your choosing." Hubbell calls the memo "typical" of the material read by some of The Eight while they were held at Plantation in the spring of 1971.[36]

Elbert, as remembered by chopper pilot Frank Anton, "was the strangest POW" in the Kushner group. "He had several stories about his capture," said Anton, one of which made Anton think he had been captured while AWOL. Anton also recalled an NLF radio broadcast that began: "My name is John Peter Johnson. I was in the Third Marine Division at Da Nang. I crossed over to the side of the Liberation Forces." POW Johnson denied that he was *that* Johnson of the radio broadcast, and was later revealed to really be Fred Elbert of New York.[37] Remembered by Daly, Elbert was "lying asleep much of the day. He'd work in spells, then suddenly be out of it, go off by himself, sometimes just sit daydreaming."[38]

ABEL LARRY KAVANAUGH

Tragically, Abel Larry Kavanaugh may have been the greatest difference-maker in the way the dissident POWs would be remembered in postwar America. His suicide by gun on June 27, 1973, put the public brakes on the efforts of Ted Guy to prosecute the radicals. Behind the scenes, on June 22, five days before Kavanaugh's death, top military lawyers had already submitted their final recommendation to drop Guy's charges against the PCs. But the abeyance of the dissidents' legal jeopardy only cleared the way for being recast as mental-health casualties of their years in captivity. Going forward, their images would be merged into the victim-veteran discourse already shaping public perceptions of antiwar GIs and veterans more generally. They weren't criminally "bad," but emotionally and psychologically wounded, traumatized.

Marine Sergeant Kavanaugh was captured near Phu Bai on April 24, 1968, after having been inadvertently left behind by the helicopters that lifted the rest of his unit back to their base camp. On the three-month trek to the Portholes camp (aka Bao Cao) he contracted malaria and dysentery.[39] Hubbell described Kavanaugh as a raucous prisoner in the Farnsworth camp who beat on cell walls and otherwise violated camp rules. He was placed in solitary confinement for five months. According to Hubbell, Kavanaugh emerged a religious convert, announcing

> he had been visiting with the Lord [and] knew himself to be a saint—"the thirteenth disciple." He insisted that he absolutely opposed the war, that he was opposed to all violence and the taking of life.[40]

Young remembered Kavanaugh as about five feet six, slight, very nice looking, with a swarthy complexion and raven-black hair.[41] He was a Chicano from Denver with a wife, Sandra, a daughter, and another child on the way when he died. He was Catholic with religious beliefs that Daly thought were "really fanatical."[42] Daly told Grant that Kavanaugh was "often hard to get along with," and like Riate, considered himself a "brown-skinned minority." And yet, Daly told Grant:

> When Kavanaugh talked about returning to the States, he imagined something that wasn't there when he left—a paradise. He talked about how he would be happy the rest of his life with his wife and little girl. . . . He talked about it all the time.[43]

With the option of a discharge after his repatriation, Kavanaugh had initially chosen instead to stay in the Corps. Apparently he had a change of mind. According to Daly, he was told that Kavanaugh

called Riate, Jane Fonda, and Cora Weiss on the day he killed himself and said he was afraid to return to the Marines. He always
thought, said Daly, that charges would be brought against the Peace
Committee and, "even if they weren't true, there would be no way we
would escape prison."[44]

Young told Grant that he was on his way to visit Kavanaugh in
Denver when he learned that he had shot himself. Young said that he
"personally felt that what [Abel] Larry did, he did for us. . . . And I
knew Larry did not want to report back to the Marines. . . . But what
he did was an attempt, I think, to take the pressure from us and put it
on the military. He gave his life for us."[45]

Kavanaugh's suicide may or may not have been the act of selfless-
ness that Young proclaimed it to be, but the Pentagon's dismissal of
the charges against the others just six days later on July 3 suggests that
his death had not been in vain. The Pentagon's press release made no
mention of Kavanaugh, stating: "The dismissals were recommended
because of lack of legally sufficient evidence and because of the policy
of the Department of Defense against holding trials for alleged propaganda statements."[46]

However, historians Rochester and Kiley allude to a more political motivation for the dismissals. Defense attorneys, they point out,
"were prepared to argue that Guy's claims were based largely on
hearsay . . . and that Guy himself had been pressured into making
concessions at Plantation." A trial would have spotlighted failings of
the accusers, such as Guy and other SROs, who were just as guilty
as those they were accusing. Dismissals of the charges, on the other
hand, would "'preserve the hero image of the returnees and diffuse
the radicals and peace groups who are looking for a cause.'"[47]

The concern of the Pentagon that the peace movement and dissident POWs would make common cause was, itself, a tacit recognition
by the higher-ups that the antiwar expressions of The Eight had been
sincere and that, though free, they were not about to recant their
commitments to peace.

Daly was angry for a long time after his discharge from the Army.
"It disturbed me," he wrote in his autobiography, "to see how people

accepted the war as being over, while Vietnamese were still being killed every day, almost 50,000 of them by the end of 1973." "More and more," he wrote, "I found myself looking toward religion again . . . the entire experience of Vietnam, even the Communist teachings, had helped me to remember a good deal of what I'd been taught long before by the Jehovah's Witnesses, and to give me a clearer idea what to do about it."[48]

Bob Chenoweth linked up with the Indochina Peace Campaign and toured the country with Tom Hayden and Jane Fonda. Riate became a folksinger, catching the attention of Irwin Silber and Barbara Dane, two legends in the radical cultural circles of the 1960s and 1970s.[49] His song "Play Your Guitars, American Friends" was recorded on a Folkways album. After working at a Veterans Administration Vets Center, he moved to the Philippines and became an activist against the regime of Ferdinand Marcos.[50] Riate died in 1984, assassinated by some accounts.[51]

ESTABLISHMENT FEARS OF A MUTUALITY between politicized POWs and the antiwar left were understandable at the time, but two developments mitigated that likelihood. One was that the antiwar movement was feeling the burnout of ten years of hitting the barricades. Splintered by sectarian infighting with a leadership that was rebalancing its political and personal priorities, it was not looking for new fronts to forge. Moreover, and notwithstanding the Hayden and Fonda overtures to POWs, the movement had been as skeptical of the dissident POWs as were the SROs—"How do we know they were not brainwashed?"

A second development was that the psychologizing of the larger population of GI and veteran war resisters was already underway when the POWs returned, and it was proving to be a more useful means of managing their political effectiveness. Why punish behavior that can be discredited, stigmatized as a mental health problem? Why criminalize dissent that can be medicalized? The road to Post-Vietnam Syndrome's acceptance as the diagnostic category PTSD was already being paved, so why not put the POWs on it along with other

Vietnam veterans? The Kavanaugh suicide, fortuitous for the military and political elites wanting to see the war in a rearview mirror, shifted the paradigm from "bad" to "mad," from villain to victim, and displaced from social memory the image of warriors, including some POWs, who turned against their war.

The history that POWs conscientiously opposed the war before and after their return from Hanoi was not so much erased or suppressed from public memory as it was displaced or overwritten by other, related story lines. The pathologizing of their dissent as a symptom of trauma was the death blow to the sense that POW dissent was conscientious. However, the psychologizing of their protest was itself a refinement of the idea that in-service, veteran, and POW resisters to the wars they were sent to fight had been misled by foreign propaganda, even "brainwashed" by the enemy. It was an idea hatched in the years after the war in Korea to explain why some U.S. POWs made statements denouncing the war, and even considered staying, or opted to stay, with their captors rather than come home when they could.

In the next two chapters we explore the trajectory of the brainwashing thesis arising out of American Cold War obsessions with communist mind-control and internal subversion, and its extension into the years of the war in Vietnam and the period that followed, during which the social memory of POW dissent would be written into obscurity.

4

The Manchurian Candidate Stalks the Homeland: Hollywood Scripts the POW Narrative

Whether cowards, opportunists, or true believers . . . the
"PCs" had become totally controlled by the enemy.
—ROCHESTER AND KILEY, *HONOR BOUND*[1]

History books, news media, memoirs, novels, film, and folklore all play roles in shaping American memory of the war in Vietnam. But few of these play more powerfully than Hollywood films and, within that medium, the images of POWs are particularly intriguing.

During the months and years of their lockup, Americans had little news about the prisoners. The trickle of letters and photographs that reached the United States raised suspicions about their verity. Who *really* wrote the letters? Were there secret messages encoded in the photographs? With nothing but their imaginations to fill in the blanks of time and place generated by the captivity of their flyers and fighters, Americans turned the Vietnam POWs into fantasy figures cast in the myths and legends passed down from previous wars. And no war played more prominently in the imagination than the one in Korea, 1950–1953. The brainwashed Korean War POW—a weak-willed traitor, a turncoat defector, a veteran *cum* mind-controlled spy and saboteur—was the archetype that could disparage antiwar POWs and veterans of the war in Vietnam, while at the same time fill theater cashboxes.

Historians Stuart Rochester and Fredrick Kiley wrote *Honor Bound* in 1998, well after the notion of brainwashing, that is, "mind control," had lost legitimacy in professional psychological literature.[2] They nevertheless dared to write what they did because associating the captives held in Asia with brainwashing was so inscribed in American culture as to be a kind of common sense, and anyone questioning it was met with ridicule. Indeed, if Rochester and Kiley had written the opposite—that dissenting POWs had acted out of principle—it is doubtful that the Naval Institute Press would have published their book.[3]

Brainwashed POWs was the paradigm, the background assumption, used by Americans for making sense out of the fragments of information they had about what went on behind the bars and walls in Hanoi. Brainwashing was the centerpiece of the Korean War backstory that U.S. pilots had taken into their Vietnam War experience: U.S. Korean War prisoners had "caved" to the persuasiveness of their captors; their confessions of war crimes and renunciations of loyalty to the homeland had *not* been coerced. Stigmatized in the press and film as collaborators, Korean War prisoners had been portrayed as men-of-weak-character whose shortcomings were derived from a permissive and hedonistic society. As an antidote for that slur, Hollywood went overboard after the defeat in Vietnam to popularize the self-aggrandizing images that senior officers made upon their release from Hanoi in 1973—*they* had distinguished themselves as real-deal tough guys who had stayed at war even when tortured.

American amnesia about the POW experience in Vietnam is a product of popular film fare and critical film studies that has been abetted by overlooking that there were divisions within the POW group, and not calling out the silence of filmmakers on class issues that bred the animosity separating the prisoners. The films through which Americans would know and remember the POW experience of the war in Vietnam were largely based on the memories of a few SROs and the conveyance of those memories, through interviews with historians and journalists, onto the desks of screenwriters.

THE MANCHURIAN CANDIDATE

The filmic narrative with torture at its core is itself not unproblematic given that it is derived from the memories of elite officers, going back to the years 1965–69 when the tortures reportedly occurred. Moreover, we know from studies of memory that the events remembered are also constructs of the expectations that the memoirist brings to the event. In the case of the Hanoi captives, those expectations were set by what the prisoners knew, or thought they knew, about what happened to prisoners in Korea, much of which, in turn, had come to them through film.

Robinson Risner tells in his memoir *The Passing of the Night* that he entered the prison experience confident he could take "anything they could dish out." He wrote, "They could torture me to death, and I would never say anything." His self-certainty was based on his Air Force survival school training and reading "fiction magazines where people had been tortured into unconsciousness and never uttered a peep. I believed without question I was as strong as they were and that I could take it."[4]

Risner doesn't say what "fiction" he had read or what the survival school curriculum included, but it is not unlikely that the lesson plans were laced with some literary enhancements. "Dubious wisdom about American Korean War POWs," concluded Craig Howes, "profoundly influenced military policy, and eventually the way many Vietnam POWs viewed their own captivity." Howes went on to cite the 1962 film *The Manchurian Candidate* as "contain[ing] the essence of received [public] opinion" that "skilled communist indoctrinators had brainwashed American soldiers into renouncing their country."

The Manchurian Candidate is based on a 1959 novel by Richard Condon in which Staff Sergeant Raymond Shaw (Laurence Harvey), captured in Korea, has been programmed by the Chinese to carry out an assassination plot in the United States after he returns home from the war. Shaw's domineering mother (Angela Lansbury) is part of the plot, and he is portrayed as too weak—even incestuously so—to resist her entreaties. Shaw's target is his mother's new husband, who is running for president. Major Bennett Marco (Frank Sinatra), who had been captured with Shaw and is unsettled by his own nightmares about the war experience, perceives the conspiracy and races to the Madison Square Garden campaign rally to stop Shaw.[5]

THE KOREAN WAR POW STORY: WRITTEN IN HOLLYWOOD OR VIENNA?

The received public opinion on Korean War POWs that inspired *The Manchurian Candidate* had its own antecedents in film fare.[6] In *The Rack* (1956), Paul Newman played Army Captain Ed Hall Jr., who came home from Korea after being held prisoner for two years. His brother Pete had been killed in the war and his father, an Army colonel played by Walter Pidgeon, is devastated to learn that Ed will be court-martialed for giving "aid and comfort to the enemy under no duress or coercion." Under questioning by his own attorney, Hall confesses to having made propaganda statements demanded by the Communists and acknowledges he suffered no physical torture prior to doing so. With his conviction seemingly assured, Hall's defense attorney then prompts Hall to recall the prison interrogations that had elicited details of the childhood anxieties that were caused by his father's coldness.

Hall: [The Communists] brought me some paper and a candle and
said I should write—but only about myself. They also questioned me. They kept me in the cellar. It was freezing. They said
I had to sign a leaflet right then or they'd leave me alone for the
rest of my life. . . . They used to come to the door and asked how I
liked being alone. I'd bite my hand to keep from answering. And,
at night, they came and said there was a letter for me. At first, I

didn't believe them because nobody wrote to me before . . . and they said it was because nobody cared for me.

Attorney: What was in that letter?

Hall: It was very short. It was from my father. He asked me why I hadn't written to him lately.

Attorney: Is that all?

Hall: No. He said my brother Pete had been killed. And at that moment I knew I couldn't hold out any more. So, I said okay, yes, I'll sign anything . . . but I gotta get some sleep and I can't be alone anymore.

Attorney: So, in other words you collapsed.

Hall: Yes.

Attorney: Now, Captain, when they had told you to write, was that in the nature of an autobiography?

Hall: Yes.

Attorney: And what was the purpose of all this? Do you know?

Hall: Trying to find out about me.

Attorney: Trying to find out something they could use? Trying to find out some special thing they could use to break you. And finally, you gave it to them, gave them the key they were looking for.

Hall: Yes.

Attorney: (Reaches for a document) Is this not a true copy of your autobiography you wrote, what you wrote after being held in miserable conditions, seeing the letter from your father, and telling them what you did in your autobiography?

Hall: Where did you get that?!

Attorney: I've marked here a passage I'd like for you to read to the court, read out loud.

Hall: No, I can't.

Judge: The witness is instructed to read.

Hall: (Reading) When I was a kid, I remember our home—

Attorney: (Interrupting Hall) We can't hear you. Your hand is covering your mouth.

Hall: (Continues to read) . . . was a place where we had to whisper, where we shut the door. My mother was sick so much she couldn't be with us. It was a lonesome time for Peter and me. We kept waiting for our mother to get well so she could be with us. Then she died. My father was away in the Army most of the time. He left us with a bulletin board with reminders on it and our housekeeper gave us a star every day if we were good and our father looked at them when he came home. Our father taught us a lot of things soldiers should know—how to keep our room neat, how to take orders, and that soldiers don't complain. As far as I remember (choking up) my father never kissed me or held us (breaking down, sobbing, unable to finish reading).

Attorney: (Picking up the document and continuing to read from it) . . . or held us or doing the other things we would see fathers doing. I never felt warmth. I'm as strict with myself as he was. I can't seem to love anybody. I love Mother but she is gone. I love my brother but he's not here. I wish my father had given me the chance to show him how much I loved him. If this loneliness can kill me, I hope it does now.

Judge: Does the defense wish to rest?

Attorney: No, your honor.

After a court recess, the prosecutor cross-examines Hall in an exchange that would lay the template for the weak-character explanation for POW collaboration and the deficiencies in American society behind it.

Prosecutor: The thing that made you collapse was loneliness—isn't that what you said?

Hall: Yes.

Prosecutor: Now this matter of loneliness interests me. I'd like to examine it a bit. Now, Captain Hall, can you tell me about some special time when the loneliness was especially bad, sometime before you went to Korea?

Hall: What do you mean? A special day or what?

Prosecutor: Yes, a special day would be fine.

Hall: Well, some days were worse than others, I guess.

Prosecutor: You mean there was no one day when the loneliness was
    just so bad you couldn't stand it? (Shouting) One day! (Softly)
    What was loneliest day of your life?

Hall: The day my mother died.

Prosecutor: The day your mother died. The autobiography you
    wrote—the Chinese found your weakness, a very lonely boy—
    they beat you with it.

"A very lonely boy"—the "boy" puts the prosecutor's words in relief.
Hall was a decorated soldier for his service in the Second World War
and had suffered a mortar wound in Korea. "Boy," uttered here, as
the camera panned the "oh-that-poor-boy" expressions on the faces
in the courtroom and focused on Hall's own childlike sniveling and
looks of shame, was clearly meant to bring "mama's boy" to mind for
the viewers. That same "boy" was called forth in 1973 when Mike
Wallace admonished Gene Wilber on CBS's *60 Minutes* with "You
weren't a child."

The Rack's contribution to the theme of young male personalities
made vulnerable to authoritarian figures might appear, a half-cen-
tury later, as remarkably creative, a manifestation of a screenwriter's
overactive imagination. In the 1950s, though, it was in step with the
efforts of social scientists to understand what had lent whole populations in Europe to follow Hitlerian leaders. The 1950 book, *The
Authoritarian Personality*, written by Theodor Adorno and others
associated with the Frankfurt School of Critical Theory, argued that
the domineering personalities commonly associated with Fascists
had their dialectical Other in the submissive personalities that fell
in the thrall of dictators. Informed by Freudian psychoanalysis, the
book gave special attention to the institution of family, the site at
which oedipal conflicts forged the personal psychologies that carried into adult life.[7]

Viewers of *The Rack* got early notice that the filmmakers were
headed in this direction when the prosecutor called to the stand a
witness who had been imprisoned with Hall. The witness testifies that
Hall had signed a compromising statement for the guards. Under

cross-examination, the witness says Hall seemed to have changed after having been separated from the others for the period when Hall was in solitary confinement. The attorney pressed the witness on the changes he observed in Hall.

Attorney: Now, did you notice any great difference in Captain Hall? Had he changed in that period?
Witness: Well, yes. He seemed terrified.
Attorney: Had you ever seen anyone as terrified to the same extent?
Witness: Some years ago, when I was very young.
Attorney: Where?
Witness: Dachau.
Attorney: Dachau. The death camp in Germany!
Courtroom: [Gasp!]

When the prosecutor objected to the implied analogy between fascist Germany and the American culture responsible for Hall's collaboration, the judge ordered it stricken from the record. But the defense attorney returned to the point in his closing argument:

Attorney: (To the Jury) Gentlemen, if there is guilt, where does it lie? In the small defect under pressure as with Captain Hall? Or do we share it? At least those of us who created a part of a generation which may collapse because we have left it uninspired, uninformed, and like Captain Hall, unprepared to go the limit. And now we must judge Captain Hall.

BEYOND *THE RACK*

It would be almost twenty years before Hollywood would begin portraying POWs from the war in Vietnam. But the die was cast in *The Rack*, which displaced to prologue the story of what happened in the POW camp, and foregrounded the story of the repatriated captive coming home to a nation skittish about the incipient corruption of post–Second World War affluence and the Cold War climate in which McCarthyite zealots looked for communists behind every door. The narrative of homefront flaccidity carried forward through *The Manchurian Candidate* and into the popular culture that would forge the mindset of military men headed for Vietnam. Thence, it is the narrative through which the American public would remember that the war in Vietnam was lost to political liberalism, permissive parenting, economic entitlements, and a pernicious feminism that sapped the national will-to-war. It was a war-at-home with the front-line running through the psyches of the captives in Hanoi just as it did through Captain Hall's.

Fifty years later, *The Rack* might be retained on lists of a few film buffs but otherwise it is forgotten. However, its all-star cast dispels doubt that it reached into the heart of America's postwar reckoning with Korea. Walter Pidgeon had won Best Actor Oscar nominations for *Mrs. Miniver* (1942) and *Madame Curie* (1943). Lee Marvin as the Army captain who testified against Hall at the trial was already an established figure in war movies and recognized for his 1953 casting with Marlon Brando in *The Wild One*. Paul Newman was just two years away from his breakout role opposite Elizabeth Taylor in *Cat on a Hot Tin Roof*.

Similar to *The Rack, Time Limit* (1957) depicted Major Harry Cargill in a cold and forlorn POW camp, brainwashed by the communists into delivering Marxist lectures to his imprisoned buddies. Speaking in a rote and mechanical fashion, Cargill's addresses signify the mind-snatching power of communist indoctrination that was the hallmark of the POW film genre well into the 1980s. As with *The Rack,* the prison camp scene is only a flashback setting for the drama of Cargill's postwar trial for collaboration, the film's main story. In the end, Cargill is relieved of charges when he is shown to have cooperated with the communists as a strategy to save his fellow POWs from execution.

Time Limit also had the star power that ensured it a wide viewership. As its protagonist Major Cargill, Richard Basehart had already played in many war movies, including the 1951 *Fixed Bayonets*. For Cargill, he was awarded a BAFTA, the British Oscar. June Lockhart, playing Mrs. Cargill, had won a 1948 Tony and was embarking on her role as Timmy Martin's mother in the *Lassie* television series. Richard Widmark as the colonel who interrogates Cargill for collaboration was a 1947 Oscar nominee, and played opposite Marilyn Monroe in the 1952 *Don't Bother to Knock*.

In the chronology of influence, the Korean War films are important first for the influence they had on the mindset that U.S. fighters took with them to Vietnam. Since many were veterans of the Korean era, it's hard to imagine they did not watch with great interest the way Hollywood represented the war and the men who fought it; the star-studded cast of a film like *The Rack* would have added to its appeal.[8] Second, Korean War film fare would influence the American film-makers who turned out the first round of films set in the years of the war in Vietnam. Third, the films' cultural framings shaped the way Americans thought about war in the post–Second World War era, which in turn provided the cues that looped back to the screenwriters looking for story lines fitting for Vietnam and the expectations of the troops training for Vietnam.

THROUGH FRENCH INDOCHINA: THE CIRCUITOUS SEGUE TO HOLLYWOOD

Most of the story lines that would characterize the Vietnam POW films were developed in the Korean War films of the 1950s. The transition from one to the other, however, was eased by some films linking story lines across temporal and spatial boundaries. *Dragonfly Squadron* (1954), for example, was set in Korea but glanced to French Indochina for riffs that may have jump-started the imaginations of pilots, filmmakers, and theatergoers of what awaited them in Vietnam: torture and spousal fidelity. Chuck Connors, already a two-sport legend for having played for both the Brooklyn Dodgers and the Boston Celtics, plays an Army captain whose unit comes to the rescue of American aid workers about to be overrun by the Chinese communists. The group's leader, Dr. Stephen Cottrell, had been pre-viously captured in French Indochina and held prisoner by the Viet

Minh; as torture, the communists there had jammed spikes under his fingernails and ruined his hands for surgery. Mistakenly reported as killed in Indochina, Cottrell is now in Korea where he unexpectedly encounters his wife, who is there with the medical aid group and romantically involved with Air Force Major Matt Brady, assigned to train Korean pilots.

The primitive savagery attributed to the Viet Minh in *Dragonfly Squadron* was game-changing because earlier films that portrayed German POW camps had depicted more passive deprivations, such as inadequate food. The physicality of those representations of camp life in Indochina may have been metaphoric for the materiality of the Second World War's ground war versus the ideological nature of the Cold War—poignantly captured in the characterization of Vietnam as "a war for hearts and minds." POW films of the Second World War era such as *Stalag 17*, moreover, presented German prison administrators as hapless bunglers presumably too dumb to know about the mind-body chemistry of physiological torment.[9] The bridge to the psychologizing of torture, crossed as it was, with the Orientalizing of its agents, also had the effect of racializing the conflict between SROs and the dissident POWs, casting the latter as race traitors as well as military turncoats.[10]

Dragonfly Squadron also may have introduced the theme of disloyal POW wives back home. Second World War films did not give wives the prominence they would get in Vietnam war films, perhaps because the two to three years of captivity in Europe and Japan was a comparatively short time compared with the as much as eight years for the first pilots shot down in Vietnam.[11]

Another movie was *The Lost Command* (1966), set in Indochina, not Korea, just after the French defeat at Dien Bien Phu in 1954, which cued the U.S. intervention in the region. It's an important film because it introduces three more story lines that will typify what will come out of Hollywood's rendition of the Vietnam POW experience: dissension within the officer ranks; the role of class background; and the lure of the racial or ethnic Other as subtext in the issues of collaboration with the enemy.

In *The Lost Command*, Lieutenant Colonel Raspeguy leads a French regiment in a last-ditch stand at Dien Bien Phu. Raspeguy is frustrated that he has not received reinforcements soon enough, forcing him to lead his men in retreat. After capture by the Viet Minh, the unit is led on a forced march before being released when the French withdrawal from Indochina is negotiated. On his return to France, Raspeguy's troop ship stops over in Algeria where he learns that the unit has been disbanded and he has been relieved of his command. Contemplating his post-military life, Raspeguy returns to the peasant village in the French mountains where he grew up. In conversation, he acknowledges the social distance between his rural peasant roots herding sheep and the French army officers he was expected to follow.

Later, Raspeguy gains an audience with a government minister to plead his case for reassignment. Entering the office, he declines the minister's invitation to sit down saying, "He learned to stand as a shepherd boy." His eyebrow raised by the remark, the minister reads from a report that the Colonel has the respect in the field of his junior officers but that he had disobeyed orders at Dien Bien Phu. "It's your superior officers with whom you can't get along, and that has to stop," the minister commands.[12] The minister offers Raspeguy a new post, leading a unit in Algeria fighting the insurgent liberation forces. Engaged in what would become famous as the Battle of Algiers, Raspeguy faces a young Algerian fighter who had fought with Raspeguy's unit in Indochina. From there, the film revolves around the ethical dilemmas posed by personal, ethnic, and national loyalties.[13]

THE FIRST AMERICAN POW FILMS SET IN VIETNAM

It is no surprise that historians interested in what happened to the American memory of dissent within the Vietnam POW population would assume that movies had something to do with it. No surprise either that their study of Hollywood influence in that important piece of history would begin with the 1987 film *Hanoi Hilton*, thinking that it was seminal in the POW-themed genre.

In fact, *Hanoi Hilton* came out fourteen years after the POWs returned and even more years after films made in 1971 first referred to POWs in Vietnam. Most of those early films dispensed with the war itself and the history of the POW experience and featured the coming-home travails of the now ex-POWs.

In *The Forgotten Man* (1971), Dennis Weaver plays Marine Lieutenant Joe Hardy, who comes home after five years as a POW to find his wife remarried and his seven-year-old daughter adopted by her new husband. The early scenes are filled with gut-wrenching father-daughter efforts to resolve the quandaries they face. The home-front betrayal encoded in his wife's infidelity fuses with Hardy's doubt that the government had tried its best to rescue the prisoners in Hanoi. Those specters of infidelity set off his paranoid responses. Now facing government authorities trying to take his daughter from him, Hardy returns to combat instincts, kidnaps his daughter, and is killed in a shootout with the police.

Welcome Home Johnny Bristol, another 1971 film, opens with Johnny Bristol held in a bamboo cage. Bristol is remembering Charles, Vermont, the idyllic small town where he grew up. Upon repatriation, Johnny is hospitalized at a Boston VA hospital where he woos his nurse, Ann, with his descriptions of Charles. As the story unfolds, however, we see that there is no Charles, Vermont, and never was. Johnny had fantasized Charles as the mythical white-picket-fence America to which he hoped to return.

Strikingly, these two early Vietnam POW films stay on the road paved by their Korean War precursors, *Time Limit* and *The Rack*, in framing their content as a coming-home story and reducing the war to background. Both were made for television, thus assuring a wider viewing than they may have received in theaters, and, in turn, increasing their influence on the just emerging postwar representations of the war-at-home narrative that will dominate the American memory of the war years. *The Forgotten Man* picks up the spousal-loyalty thread left by *The Dragonfly Squadron*, and *Welcome Home Johnny Bristol* writes the subtext, albeit through Johnny's war-borne psychosis, that the Norman Rockwell America from which GIs departed for Vietnam was rotting, due to its discard of traditional values.

Although these two films were released two years before the wholesale repatriation of the 591 Hanoi prisoners—too early for them to have touched on the story of dissent within the prison population— they ignored completely the figures of GIs who had been captured in the South years earlier and returned home opposed to the war. These early films could have featured, for example, ex-POW George Smith, who was released in 1965 after two years of captivity in the South and wrote *P.O.W.: Two Years with the Viet Cong* about having come to consciousness about the war during captivity. Or they could have told the stories of James Jackson, Dan Pitzer, and Edward Johnson, who were freed by antiwar activist Tom Hayden in 1967 only to return home to face charges that they had been brainwashed.[14] Rather than presage the fact that the Peace Committee, the hard core of the Hoa Lo dissenters, was composed of GIs captured in the South and forge a new template for the POW narrative, filmmakers ignored the story.[15]

POWs, THE NEW LEFT, AND THE BURDEN OF BRAINWASH

The exclusion of the dissident POWs from Hollywood story lines was not a given. After all, antiwar veterans who had not been POWs would soon be marqueed in the 1978 *Coming Home*, starring Jon Voight. His character Luke comes out against the war while recovering from wounds in a VA hospital. But *Coming Home* was an exception, the explanation for which illuminates the complexities surrounding the cultural representations of the POW dissenters.[16]

Coming Home was the project of actress Jane Fonda, who had gotten involved with uniformed war resisters and antiwar veterans while living in Paris in the mid-1960s. When she returned to the States for good in 1969, she became an ardent supporter of the GI Coffeehouse Movement and helped fund the 1971 Winter Soldier Hearings into U.S. war crimes. In short, Fonda's star power and financial resources gave Vietnam Veterans Against the War (VVAW) the media visibility and celebrity imprimatur that magnetized its reputation and drew thousands more Americans to the cause of ending the war. Antiwar veterans were a hot ticket for the movement and the box office—unless they had spent their Vietnam years in Hoa Lo prison.

The antiwar POWs were not the darlings of the antiwar movement that the whistleblowers of the Winter Soldier Hearings had become. In the first place, most were pilots who had rained hell on the Vietnamese. And second, most were old enough and well enough educated to have known better than to have committed the airborne atrocities they did—or they should have known better. The antiwar statements made by dissident pilots, moreover, came *after* their bombing raids left civilians terrified and North Vietnam's urban infrastructure shredded, a fact that hardly burnished their sincerity. Most of the dissident POWs were not pilots, of course, but the pilots were clearly the stars of the coming-home show, making "guilt by association" (with them) a kind of collateral jeopardy borne by the others: *all* these guys are professional killers undeserving of sympathy or solidarity went a line of left-wing thinking.[17]

Additionally, war opponents were as inhibited by Cold War fantasies of communist brainwashing as anyone else. Had some captured pilots really come out against the war? Or had their statements been coerced? Had they been brainwashed? And would a peace activist quoting a recalcitrant POW be dismissed as a communist dupe—brainwashed? Would a left-wing acceptance into the movement of the antiwar POWs be spun by the Right as proof that the movement was a front for International Communism?[18]

This is the kind of Cold War baggage carried by peace travelers to Hanoi. Their meetings in Hanoi with captive pilots would be seminal in forming each group's impressions of the others.[19]

PEACE TRAVELERS MEET THE POWs

Carol McEldowney and Vivian Rothstein kept journals on their 1967 trip to Vietnam. McEldowney had been active in SDS at the University of Michigan; she was present at the Port Huron retreat where the SDS manifesto, known as the *Port Huron Statement*, was written. In 1964, she moved to Cleveland to work with the SDS community-organizing project, ERAP (Economic Research and Action Project). Rothstein had gone to UC Berkeley and been involved in the Free Speech Movement. After civil rights organizing in Jackson, Mississippi, in summer of 1965, she joined the ERAP campaign in Chicago.[20]

In 1967, McEldowney and Rothstein were invited by SDS leader Tom Hayden to attend a conference in Bratislava, Czechoslovakia, that brought U.S. antiwar activists together with representatives of the North Vietnamese government and the National Liberation Front (NLF). As the conference ended, the Vietnamese invited Hayden and six other Americans to visit North Vietnam. McEldowney and Rothstein were among the six.[21]

McEldowney's journal is speckled with signs that "brainwashing" weighed heavily on the minds of the Hayden delegation. On her fifth day in Hanoi she wondered if the cultural panic surrounding communism in the United States would taint whatever her delegation reported upon return to the States: "For me (for us?) the problem will be to learn to communicate what we've learned to people in the U.S. without seeming brainwashed."[22]

The contemplation of self-censorship lest their testimonies be dismissed as biased was difficult, but the specter of brainwashing presented the travelers with a still more pernicious face. The New Left, of which SDS was the central component, and to which the Hayden delegation was fundamentally committed, had itself been born out of dissatisfaction with communists who had dominated its Old Left predecessor, the Communist Party of the United States, the very communists publicly reviled for simple-minded servility to the Soviet Union and the practice of mind control within its organization. With those strains of Cold War anti-communism coursing through its own veins, the Hayden delegation faced a dilemma: how to keep their guard up against expected attempts by their communist hosts to brainwash *them* while simultaneously processing their experiences for presentation at home in a way that challenged public paranoia about communist duplicity and mind control. "All of us must avoid doing what the pro-Soviet people [in the CPUSA] did in the 1930s," McEldowney wrote in her journal, before adding that their public presentations would have to acknowledge their "awareness of some the restrictions and less attractive characteristics [of communism]."

The Americans went into their meeting with POWs suspicious of both their Vietnamese hosts and the prisoners. Would the prison administration try to prettify the prison conditions with testimonies coerced from the prisoners? Were the prisoners handpicked for interviews because they had been brainwashed or terrified into mouthing the communists' line? "We had a lot of discussions about whether the pilots were truthful—were they really treated well or were they being forced to pretend?" Little did they know that the prisoners were suspicious of them, lest they had been brainwashed by the communists. Sailor Doug Hegdahl, who had been captured in May, asked the delegation several times, wrote McEldowney, "who sent us, who financed us, and whether we were communists."

In the end, the Cold War infection of their own political perspectives may have been the insurmountable barrier to leftist affinity with the antiwar POWs.

The Bratislava group met Air Force pilot Larry Carrigan on October 12, 1967; he had been captured just a month before meeting the group. In her journal, Rothstein wrote:

> [Carrigan] asked us why we [are] against the war—we said because Saigon gov. is not what VN people want, that it is brutal & we have no right to be here.
>
> He said he agreed. That he really knew very little about VN before he came here.
>
> Said we should go home & not be belligerent but try to talk to the Amer. people & explain abt. the Geneva Accords.

"After we spoke to pilots," wrote Rothstein, "Tom [Hayden] tried to explain that it was very 'disturbing' because we didn't know what to believe of what the pilots said or how to use it as propaganda back home." She continued: "Tom didn't say exactly what he meant—that he was sure the prisoners were treated well & that they are not getting brainwashed but that we think pilots who are as anti-war now as Carrigan are talking like that because they've been taught to by the Air Force once captured that they are not politically more aware."

Hayden's twist on the POWs' veracity is eye-catching, but McEldowney's record of the Carrigan interview minces fewer words:[23]

After a while, I didn't believe anything he said (and I withdrew). . . . I really hated him—saw him as the white guy from the Southwest who would drop bombs on negroes in a race riot.[24]

A few lines later, she wrote, "I felt for the first time that we were being *used* by [the communists]."

Following the meeting, Rothstein summarized her feelings:

The experience was rather awful. We all fell into a closeness with the pilots on the basis of being Americans—we forgot where we were and who we were. Not until the middle of Carrigan's talk did I realize not to trust what he said at all. I felt a little like I was in the *Manchurian Candidate*—with the oriental communists around us and us in the situation of being brainwashed. It was caused by all the stereotypes I've ever known [and heard] about Chinese and Korean communists and their brainwashing.

McEldowney also inserted notes from John "Jock" Brown's diary in her journal. Brown was a minister who had joined the group in Czechoslovakia. Amid rambling notes about Carrigan's views about antiwar demonstrations—he said they were "great" but questioned their effectiveness—and the need to educate Americans about the Geneva Accords, Brown recorded the following:

Question for Carrigan from Vivian (Rothstein): "Will they say you've been brainwashed?"

Carrigan: "I don't know what the military will say, but do I seem
    brainwashed (laugh)? I was never brainwashed."

LEFT BEHIND: REBEL POWS ON THE
CUTTING-ROOM FLOOR

With no antiwar Left to nurture the political capital of dissenting
POWs who returned home, and no Jane Fonda to champion them,
the POW story would be hijacked by the political Right to stir public
unsettledness about "what really happened over there." The Right's
agenda to feed suspicions that the government was not telling the
truth about the war as they cast aspersions on the loyalty of the antiwar movement was prelude to the revanchism of the Ronald Reagan
presidency that would popularize the paranoia about "Washington
insiders" as seditious fifth columnists. Hollywood's contribution to
that agenda would be twofold: first, displace the image of the dissenting POWs, and eventually all real-life POWs, with that of mythical
POWs abandoned by the government and left behind in Southeast
Asia; and second, recast the image of radical veterans from the
political problem they were into a mental health problem.[25] Wilber,
Chenoweth, and their brothers-against-the-war who had formed
Vietnam Veterans Against the War years earlier, were better understood as traumatized victims than as warriors transformed into
peacemakers by their experience in Vietnam.

Hollywood's disinterest in the story of peacemaking POWs is
understandable. The Cold War hysteria about brainwashing that
was ginned in Korean War films like *The Rack* and *The Manchurian
Candidate* was now blowback that inhibited artistic and market-
ing judgments about what the theater-going public would pay for.
Intimations that not all the POWs had come home dampened interest in the accused collaborators and even their hardcore accusers. The
POW *du jour* was the one unacknowledged by the government and
forgotten by the public, the one who did not come home.

A spate of films made after 1973 featured the coming-home travails
of the now ex-POWs: *Mr. Majestyk* (1973), *Rolling Thunder* (1977),

Ruckus (1980), and *Some Kind of Hero* (1981), all following that pattern. That it took four years before the first explicitly POW-themed film would be made, in 1977, suggests that Hollywood needed time to digest the loss of the war and decide what to do with the POW story.[26]

Good Guys Wear Black in 1977 made a statement: the government had abandoned POWs in Southeast Asia; the war was not over so we—veterans, now citizen-soldiers—would have to go back, rescue the POWs, and finish the job. The raiders, arriving at a bamboo-prison compound emptied of prisoners—but occupied by Viet Cong ambushers—have been set up, a betrayal blamed on Washington by the unit's leader. Metaphorically, this stab-in-the-back given to the mission contributes to the betrayal narrative for the loss of the war then building in the country, while the motif of duplicity that enveloped it primed a public inclination to view POW dissenters as traitors.

Uncommon Valor (1983) followed suit. A television news report in the background tells listeners that 2,500 POWs are still unaccounted for and "until they're all back . . . the war will never be over." Washington is doing nothing; Col. Jason Rhodes (Gene Hackman) thinks his son Frank is alive among the missing; with the backing of a rich donor, he assembles a unit of Vietnam veterans to go searching for Frank. Trekking into Laos, the unit arrives in a decimated village where it finds only the skeletons of its inhabitants said to have been gassed. Further on, a POW camp is raided but Frank is not among those brought home.[27]

As a genre, the POW/MIA films consolidated Nietzschean themes flowing from 1950s films such as *The Rack* that called out the effeminized post–Second World War culture that had sapped American will-to-war. Filmic images of POWs languishing in bamboo cages were metaphors for the American greatness and masculinity lost in Vietnam that awaited recovery and return. Ronald Reagan's proclamation that "government is the problem, not the solution" was a call to arms for avenging Ramboesque vigilantes who could counterweight the tax-paying public's reluctance to fight again: the "Vietnam Syndrome." Reagan's signature slogan—"It's morning in America"— summoned the back-to-the-future sentiments seeking restoration of a prelapsarian America whose men had been waylaid by the women's movement, whose work ethic had been eroded by government entitlements, and whose pride in the military victories of the Second World War had been insulted by the antiwar movement and the Vietnam veterans associated with it.[28]

THE POW-RESCUE AND MIA-recovery films were not a departure from the brainwashing story line of *Manchurian Candidate* fare that dated back to the post–Korean War years. Rather, the screenwriters took the psychological premises of brainwashing beyond the colloquial expression of "psychologizing the political," popular in the early 1970s, and created a new diagnostic category initially known as "post–Vietnam syndrome" and later as Post Traumatic Stress Disorder (PTSD). Cast in film as captives to be found and rescued, POWs were rendered as passive victims or even hapless losers who needed saving by fantasy figures cut by Sylvester Stallone's Rambo and Chuck Norris's Colonel Braddock.

Written out of Hollywood scripts and, going forward, out of public memory, representations of dissident POWs would be dissolved into the larger set of antiwar veterans that cultural workers, journalists, and psychiatrists were busy pathologizing as mental and emotional casualties of war who were more deserving of sympathy than solidarity.

5

Damaged, Duped, and Left Behind: Displacing POW Dissent

y the end of the 1970s, Vietnam veterans were commonly portrayed in film and news reports as casualties of the war, their military mission sold out on the home front and their homecoming marked by ingratitude and condemnation. Representations of POWs followed a similar path. The hero-prisoner imaging that had dominated the news through Operation Homecoming soon faded as a war-fatigued public turned to affairs it had put aside for the draft, service, and protests against the war.

What interest there was in POW dissenters merged into the mental health discourse that was medicalizing GI and veteran dissent as symptomatic. It was trauma, not politics and conscience, that moved in-service resisters. If there was energy for the war after 1973, it was mustered by conspiratorial rightists around the myth that some POWs had been left behind as Washington exited Vietnam.

MEDICALIZING DISSENT

The template for the representation of POW dissidents had been forged by news organizations and mental health professionals in their coverage and treatment of the veterans who had already come out against the war by the time POWs arrived home.

In-service resistance had been rife since the war's earliest years. That resistance was expressed through claims to conscientious objection, refusals to deploy, collaboration with civilian peace activists at off-base coffeehouses, and efforts to organize opposition through the GI Press, a network of antiwar newspapers. In Vietnam, war resisters displayed antiwar symbols on clothing, sabotage of equipment, refusals to carry out orders, and acts of violence against superiors, known as fragging.[1]

Unsurprisingly, authorities in and outside the military sought to prevent, disrupt, and punish acts of dissension. GI coffeehouses were declared off-limits and raided by local police, radical newspapers were confiscated, peace symbols were banned, their wearing punished as Article 15 violations, and court-martial charges were brought against the most serious offenders. Predictably, attempts to suppress dissent bred more misbehavior, and by the last years of the war the low level of troop discipline threatened military operations.[2]

Officially, the military denied that it had a problem. The investigative reports it commissioned on the problem in 1970 and 1971 were not made available until after the war. Journalists were dispatched to Vietnam to find and report *war* stories, not *antiwar* stories. Until veterans returned with eyewitness accounts of breakdowns in unit discipline that might be affecting operations, news organizations either remained oblivious to the emerging rebellion or ignored it.[3]

But the news came out. In early May 1969, the news service UPI carried a lengthy report on the GI antiwar movement that included photographs of coffeehouse scenes and stories from underground GI newspapers. On May 23, *Life* featured a story about what it called "a widespread new phenomenon in the ranks of the military: *public dissent.*" In August, the New York *Daily News* reported the refusal of an infantry unit in Vietnam to continue fighting. On November 9, the *New York Times* ran a full-page advertisement that was signed by 1,365 GIs opposing the war and included the rank and duty station of each signer.[4]

That the American people knew all of this as it happened under-scores several questions: What happened between then and now? What happened to the awareness and memory of such widespread resistance to the war within the military?

The answers to those questions help explain the expurgation of POW resisters from public memory. In the closing years of the war, establishment leaders began to worry about the legacy left by a gen-eration of warriors who turned against their war. In short form, the Nixon administration, news organizations, and leading cultural insti-tutions—Hollywood filmmakers in particular—endeavored to cast shade on the authenticity and reliability of their dissent.

OSTRACIZING DISSENT

The April 15, 1967, mobilization against the war, known as "Spring Mobe," had brought together six veterans to form Vietnam Veterans Against the War. The VVAW presence six months later at the October March on the Pentagon and support for the 1968 presidential cam-paign of antiwar candidate Eugene McCarthy established the group as a powerful voice for peace in Vietnam. Unable to directly suppress and punish dissenting views, the Nixon White House and its pro-war minions sought instead to drive a wedge between the radical veterans and the liberal majority in the antiwar movement.

Early efforts to do that took the form of ostracism, defaming pro-testing veterans as traitors and even communists. When VVAW members marched from Morristown, New Jersey, to Valley Forge, Pennsylvania, to protest the war in September 1970, older veterans of previous wars and stalwarts of Nixon's Republican Party base belittled them for their long hair and shouted for them to "go back to Hanoi!"[5]

In April 1971, VVAW staged an encampment on the National Mall in Washington to accompany its lobbying effort to end the war. John Kerry, representing VVAW, gave a passionate antiwar speech before a congressional committee for which he was later accused of betray-ing the security of the troops still in Vietnam. A year later, efforts to criminalize VVAW peaked when charges were brought against the

Gainesville, Florida, chapter for planning an armed attack on the 1972 Republican Party national convention in Miami Beach.[6]

DISCREDIT THEIR AUTHENTICITY

The widespread distrust of information flowing from Washington about the war meant that the voices from the ground level view of returned veterans were welcomed by the American public, but they were threatening to political and military elites. If those voices could not be suppressed or isolated, they would have to be discredited, their identity disputed, their authenticity impugned.

Beyond the crude suggestion that VVAW members might be agents of a hostile government and criminalized as seditious, critics suggested that protesting veterans were not "authentic," their numbers inflated by radicals posing as veterans. Speaking before a military audience in May of 1971, Vice President Spiro Agnew said he did not know how to describe the VVAW members encamped on the Mall but "heard one of them say to the other: 'If you're captured . . . give only your name, age, and the phone number of your hairdresser.'"[7]

In the same speech, Agnew said the antiwar vets "didn't resemble" the veterans "you and I have known," a statement, when combined with having gay-baited them, was an effort to draw an "us and them" distinction. Thusly drawn, the line invited more pronounced distinctions between "real men" and those who now refused to fight.

STIGMATIZING AS PATHOLOGICAL

Ostracizing and Otherizing are forms of stigmatizing, the denigration of an individual or group's identity. In his 1964 book *Stigma*, sociologist Erving Goffman wrote that the attribution of stigma can disqualify those "Others" from full social acceptance. In modern society, assignment of mental illness to targeted parties has become a powerful and pervasive form of stigmatizing.[8]

The first unlawful break-ins leading to the Watergate scandal of 1973 were those done by President Richard Nixon's "plumbers" on the psychiatrist's office of Daniel Ellsberg. A Marine Corps veteran and employee of the Rand Corporation in contract work for the government, Ellsberg had copied secret documents showing that political and military leaders had been misleading the public on the conduct of the war for years; the documents were later known as "The Pentagon Papers." Ellsberg had released the Papers to the press in 1971, incurring the wrath of the president. Wanting to discredit Ellsberg prior to the 1972 elections, Nixon assembled a team of former FBI and CIA agents to burglarize the doctor's office for files that would "destroy [Ellsberg's] public image."[9]

At the same time as the plumbers' raid on the psychiatrist's office, the press was hanging the same mental health markers on VVAW actions. When VVAW gathered in Miami Beach to protest the Republican Party's nomination of Richard Nixon as its presidential candidate in 1972, the *New York Times* featured a front-page story on the mental problems of Vietnam veterans. Beneath a headline reading "Postwar Shock Besets Ex-GIs" was a report peppered with words and phrases like "psychiatric casualty," "mental health disaster," "emotional illness," and "mental breakdown." The story acknowledged that there was little hard research on which to base those characterizations. Indeed, if the reporter had done his homework, he probably would have found Peter Bourne's 1970 book, *Men, Stress, and Vietnam*, in which Bourne, an Army psychiatrist in Vietnam, reported American personnel having suffered the lowest psychiatric casualty rate in modern warfare.[10]

After the 1972 *Times* story, the press tapped out a steady beat of stories about soldiers home from Vietnam with psychological derangements. In this, journalism was in step with the direction in which popular culture was headed with its representations of the war and the people who fought it. Hollywood had begun portraying Vietnam veterans as damaged goods since the mid-1960s and, consequentially, writing political veterans out of their stories. Films like *Blood of Ghastly Horror* (1965) and *Motorpsycho* (1965) anticipated the symptomatology of Post-Traumatic Stress Disorder before health care professionals coined the phrase. Controversies over the validity of war trauma nomenclature riled professional organizations throughout the late 1970s, and when PTSD was finally affirmed as a diagnostic category in the *Diagnostic and Statistical Manual of the American Psychiatric Association* in 1980, one of the authors of the terminology, Chaim Shatan, credited a *New York Times* opinion piece with having been the difference-maker in professionals' deliberations of its merit.

The shift from the political discourse that had dominated the veterans' homecoming story in the late 1960s and early 1970s to the mental health story line that became dominant in the 1980s is evinced in Hollywood film. In the 1978 film *Coming Home*, Luke (Jon Voigt) is politicized by his experience in Vietnam and shoddy treatment at a military hospital; he comes out publicly against the war. Four years later, we're given Rambo (Sylvester Stallone), who suffers flashbacks to the bamboo cage that confined him as a POW and then goes on a murderous rampage. Although political veterans like Luke were never prominent in feature films, the die was cast with Rambo. From then on, American filmgoers got a regular diet of warriors returning home with hurts, the unrepentant POW peacemakers among them.

More than the historical record itself, it would be the voices of veterans testifying to what they had done and seen that would shape public memory of the war and the POWs would be pulled into that agenda.

THE FORGOTTEN POW DISSENTERS

The POW story is as complicated and conflicted as that of the rest of the Vietnam-generation of veterans. The peace agreement that ended the war on January 27, 1973, stipulated the arrangements for the release of U.S. POWs, most of them held in prisons in and around Hanoi. The releases began on February 12 and continued in three increments until March 29. Carried aboard Air Force C-141 aircraft, they landed first at Clark Air Force Base in the Philippines for debriefing and medical assessment. From Clark, they were flown to stateside bases and on to regional hospitals and their hometowns.

News coverage of the POWs' arrival at Clark anticipated stories of dissent behind the bars that were yet to come. "Freed P.O.W. Asserts He Upheld U.S. Policy" read a February 15 *New York Times* headline before reporting that the pilot had made statements opposing the war while being held. A February 23 headline, "P.O.W.s Maintained Discipline but Had Some Quarrels and Were Split on the War," promised still more.

Intriguing as these headlines seem now, they may have been less so for readers in 1973. Peace activists and journalists had been journeying to Hanoi for years, where they met with POWs and heard a range of views about the war. George Smith, captured in the South and released in 1965, had written a book, *P.O.W.*, about his two years in captivity that was critical of the war. Far more interesting in retrospect is how widespread knowledge about POW dissenters in 1973 has been forgotten. As with the lost history of GI and veteran dissent recounted above, the story of POW dissent is less about forgetting than the reconstruction of what is remembered.[11]

"MUZZLED POWS . . ."

Not a salvo from an ACLU broadside, the headline "Muzzled POWs," replete with an ellipsis, topped a *New York Times* editorial—not an op-ed—on February 24, 1973. It followed a set of stories carried on its own pages about attempts to suppress news coverage of POWs' dissent since their release twelve days earlier. "P.O.W. Conduct Barred as Topic" read a February 5 headline a week before the first releases; "Managing the P.O.W.s: Military Public Relations Men Filter Prisoner Story" on February 20 told of eighty public relations specialists assembled to "hide possible warts and stand as a filtering screen between the press and the story."

Dissent had been a fact of life inside the walls of Hoa Lo for at least two years before the POWs' release and, not unlike their counterparts in leadership across the U.S. military system, the Senior Ranking Officers in the Hanoi prison system came down hard on those who deviated from the party line; efforts to suppress the protests included threats of courts-martial and even violence against them when they were released and returned to the States.

When outright suppression didn't work, the SROs warned others to stay away from the radicals, trying to isolate the bad apples. The prison administrators and guards controlled the movement and communications among the prisoners, of course, but the SROs contrived their own kangaroo command hierarchy into which they tried, first, to co-opt the highest-ranking dissidents, Navy Captain Walter Eugene Wilber and Marine Lieutenant Colonel Edison Miller, and, failing that, relieve them of military authority—"excommunicated" them, as historian Craig Howes put it. From then on, wrote Howes, "most men avoided them like the devil."[12]

The demonizing of the dissidents through "excommunication" is a recognizable form of ostracism, the same tactic as that implemented against the GI and veterans' antiwar groups in the States. By exiling the leaders, the SROs had set them up for victim-blaming. Their social exclusion would be construed by their peers (and later by the American public) as self-exacted, a kind of asked-for segregation, the responsibility for which lay with them. Putatively, the irrationality of their behavior stemmed from personal traits. They were loners, losers, alienated, and maladjusted, a cluster of shortcomings bespeaking weak character.[13]

The "weakness" notion was a form of slander, but it gained currency through its assignment to the ground troops captured in the South who arrived at the Hanoi complex in spring of 1971. Some of them were part of what was known as the Kushner group; many were younger enlisted men and lesser educated than the high-ranking pilots who preceded them into the Hanoi lockups; and the group was disproportionately non-white.[14] The ascription of personal failings to the Kushners' and other enlisted prisoners' antiwar leanings and resistance to the SROs' chain of command was a way to discredit the political authenticity of their opposition. Notwithstanding the condescension of rooting those "weaknesses" in the rebels' social backgrounds, the weakness language was also the rhetoric of character assassination. It dog whistled *moral* weakness, a failure to profess patriotic faith by willingness to suffer worldly deprivation. With a twist, it riffed on the mental health discourse already forming the narrative of GI and veteran dissent in which the voices of conscience, home from Hanoi, would fit.

The disrespect shown for the antiwar POWs followed them in their return home. From their first landing at Clark Air Force Base in the Philippines, through the White House welcoming staged for the POWs, their representation in the press, and further on in the stack of books that would be written about the "POW experience," they were the deviants whose behavior needed to be accounted for and explained.

FROM MUZZLED, TO CRIMINAL, TO MEDICAL: THE TRANSFORMING NARRATIVE OF POW DISSENT

Forgetting is an insidious process because it creates its own obscurity even as it takes place. In the case of the POW dissidents, the news about their censoring was short-lived, replaced first by stories about legal charges brought against them, and their defense against those charges. It was a kind of reversing-the-verdict maneuver whereby the stories about muzzled POWs that had the government on the defensive for the violation of freedom of speech were now reversed, putting the dissidents on the defensive for their conduct as prisoners.

Most news stories in March carried headlines like Seymour Hersh's for the *New York Times* on March 16, 1973: "Eight May Face Courts-Martial for Antiwar Roles as P.O.W.s." It was not as though the POWs were silenced by that spin so much as being compelled to speak as defendants in interviews with news reporters. This conflict was on display in Mike Wallace's interview with Gene Wilber on April 1. Confronted with Wallace's inference that he must have caved to the fear of torture—the "weakness" narrative that was building in the press—Wilber stuck with his claim to "conscience and morality." Wilber's stand effectively turned the tables again, putting the prosecutorial parties on the defensive for suppressing conscience.[15] Wilber's adherence to principle, however, was a grain of sand in the celebratory tide raising the stature of the "good" POWs reputed to have pridefully endured the "torture" handed out by their communist captors.

The POW news in May 1973 was dominated by President Richard Nixon's White House reception for them and their families. Press coverage of the reception totally erased the antiwar POWs from the story, and worse, did not cover the intimidations and threats exacted on them and their families behind the scenes.[16]

Legal maneuvering returned in the wake of the White House reception when Stockdale charged Wilber and Miller in late June. Wilber, through his appointed defense attorney, Lieutenant Commander Ronald M. Furdock, argued that the statements he made were not a violation of the UCMJ,[17] and that he and Stockdale had never met. Nor had Wilber met the "witnesses" listed as having knowledge of his "criminal" acts. Despite repeated attempts, Wilber's defense team was never permitted to interview the witnesses, some of whom also had never met Wilber. The allegations were rumors, hearsay that had been spread through the tap code.

The tap code was a Morse Code–like means of communication used by the POWs during periods of isolation. By tapping on the prison walls separating them, they maintained a bit of contact. Words were spelled by tapping two-character representations of a five-by-five matrix for each letter of the alphabet. Thus, row 1, column 1 was letter *A* (tap...tap); row 1, column 2 was *B* (tap...tap, tap). Messaging was slow, terse, and filled with abbreviations—not a forum for detail and nuance. Furthermore, messages were passed from room to room through adjacent walls from memory, a method that invited revisions and omissions, a form of "whisper down the lane" with no checks on accuracy. John Dramesi remembered the tap code as being a form of entertainment with lots of pornographic humor and gossip.[18]

Wilber and his attorneys were confident that the whispered communications in encounters in washrooms and limited communications through the tap code were the primary "witness" to his alleged crimes. These types of gossip communications were not going to stand up to the rules of evidence required in courts-martial, but they survive as the core of the "liberal dupe" slander that persists through-out the hero-prisoner narrative.

The likelihood of successful prosecution was slim. The Marine Corps had determined that "the case could not be successfully prosecuted."[19] The Commandant of the Marine Corps (regard-ing Miller) and the Judge Advocate General of the Navy (regarding Wilber) both recommended to Secretary of the Navy Warner that the charges against Miller and Wilber be dropped. Warner had made a three-month investigation of the charges before dismissing them; a court-martial would be disruptive to those who would have to testify, he said. In September 1973, he issued letters of censure to Wilber and Miller, charging them with failing to meet the standards expected of officers of the armed forces and announced they would be retired in "the best interests of the naval service." Ignoring that the government had a weak case that would not likely lead to conviction, Rochester and Kiley spun the dismissal of charges as an act of leniency extended to the "guilty" Miller and Wilber.[20]

By the time the legal case against Wilber and Miller collapsed, the dominant narrative had turned again. The rebels weren't criminal so much as emotionally and psychologically hurt, sick, damaged goods, just as were others of their ilk who had been in the streets as protesters against the war since 1967. A June 2 New York Times story headlined "Ex-P.O.W.s to Get Health Counseling for 5-Year Period," sprinkled in references to "high violent death rates," "depression," "fright," and "euphoria," with no references to sources for the claims. "Some Wounds Are Inside: Health of P.O.W.s" headlined a June 10 health column, raising mental health as the specter that would stigmatize dissent as a symptom. A July 15 story, "Antiwar P.O.W.s: A Different Mold Seared by the Combat Experience," locked in the mental health discourse despite there being virtually nothing in the content of the article to support the use of "seared" in the headline.[21]

The psychologizing of the dissenting views within the POW popu-lation was a way to dismiss their authenticity as political and moral expressions of conscience.

As it turned out, some never-say-die rightists who believed the war was not yet over, much less lost, were not about to have their disgust with POW dissenters salved with medical compassions. For them, Wilber, Miller, and the peacenik Eight were traitors—and there may have been more to what went on in Hoa Lo, and beyond, than what was known. Had everyone forgotten *The Manchurian Candidate*?

POWs OR MIAs?: THE NATIONAL LEAGUE OF FAMILIES BLENDS THE IDENTITIES

Throughout the late 1950s and early 1960s, there were a smattering of U.S. military and CIA personnel captured in Laos and Vietnam, but the purpose of their presence there was never clear, and they were all quickly released. The first captive who was on an acknowledged combat mission, as an "advisor," was taken in 1961. From then on, wrote historian Bruce Franklin, the number rose, but it was not until 1969, he says, that POWs became an issue.

According to Franklin, the revelations in 1968 that Americans had slaughtered civilians at My Lai and that the Phoenix program was arresting and assassinating suspected leaders of the National Liberation Front triggered President Richard Nixon to make an issue out of the way the communists were treating "our" prisoners. More pointedly, journalist Don Luce exposed in a February 1969 *Christian Century* article that tiger cages on Con Son Island held purported communists who were captured by the United States.[22] These exposés of American complicity in atrocities threatened to erode already sagging public support for the war as well as open government and military officials to charges of war crimes. As a counter-propaganda move on May 19, 1969, Nixon initiated what became known as the "Go Public" campaign to use U.S. prisoners held by the communists to leverage public opinion against the Hanoi government.

Nixon was also under pressure from the wives of POW pilots who had been frustrated by the outgoing Johnson administration's reticence on the POW issue. James Stockdale's wife, Sybil, was set in motion by a September 1, 1968, article in the *San Diego Union* newspaper titled "Red Brain Wash Teams Work on US Pilots." Mrs.

Stockdale had "pored over" books on the Korean War POW experience such as "*In Every War But One,*" the Eugene Kincaid 1959 book that was an inspiration for *The Manchurian Candidate*.[23] Her reading had her worrying that government insiders were "too friendly with those Americans who happily spread North Vietnamese propaganda in the United States." She sent the *San Diego Union* article to Secretary of Defense Clark Clifford and Ambassador W. Averell Harriman and asked "what steps are being taken to prevent" these mistreatments of prisoners. When Harriman replied to her with assurance that the welfare of the prisoners was "uppermost in his mind," she later recalled her skepticism of his sincerity.[24]

Nixon's election in November opened a path for Mrs. Stockdale's access to the White House, and she took it. In July 1969, POW wives formed the National League of Families of American Prisoners in Southeast Asia with her as its head. The "League," as it became known, received funding support from the Republican National Committee, and RNC "advisors" helped coordinate its activities, according to Franklin.[25]

The League of Families lobbied the Nixon administration to negotiate the release of prisoners. The White House, however, embedded the prisoner release issue in its negotiations to withdraw troops from Vietnam and end the war. The U.S. military assaults would continue until the prisoners were released. The North Vietnamese were equally adamant—no peace, no releases.

The three-way stalemate over the POW issue continued until the last months of 1972 and was tightened by the League's demands that U.S. personnel missing in action (MIAs) be included in the negotiations. Questions arose immediately over who was known to be a captive and who was known to be missing—and *maybe* held captive. The wives of some pilots had been told their husbands had been shot down but were "missing." The absence of further information raised suspicions that the North Vietnamese were holding some pilots as prisoners but not admitting it. In fact, says Franklin, some of the missing were known by the Defense Department to have died in the shootdowns but their remains were unrecovered. The Defense

Department, he found, kept two sets of books: an undisclosed account that separated POWs from those known to be missing but BNR, or Bodies not Recovered, and a public account that lumped POWs and MIAs together.[26]

Unaccounted for or missing fighters are the sources of great anxiety for loved ones who have little more than their imaginations for filling in the blanks of the unknowns created by the separations. The unknowns also fuel the myths and legends that surround MIA issues. One of the greatest of those is the Legend of the Lost Command, born in the First World War's Battle of the Argonne Forest: a patrol went out and did not return. What happened to them? Were they lost? Were they captured? Were they dead? Had they deserted or defected to the enemy? Later it was revealed that a group in the unit had gone AWOL and ended up in German hands. When only one member of that group, an army private, returned, public suspicions raced to thoughts of treason and betrayal.[27]

The MIA soldiers, Marines, and pilots held in Vietnam were figures of no less fascination and, with Cold War intrigues factored in, speculation about the whats and wherefores surrounding them grew with time. Were the Vietnamese lying about who they held captive? Was Washington denying knowledge about some of the missing for reasons of mission security? How many, known to be dead, were still counted as POW/MIA by the Defense Department, a cruel use of information that kept their families in a painful state of suspended animation? Might some of the ground troops missing in the South have deserted—or even gone over to the other side, like the Peace Committee signees of Al Riate's proposal to do just that?

H. ROSS PEROT

The public's interest in the MIAs made it an immanently exploitable topic for political and ideological purposes. Just days after Richard Nixon's election in November, Texas multimillionaire H. Ross Perot funded full-page newspaper advertisements picturing children pleading for the return of their daddys being held in Hanoi. Perot was a

Naval Academy graduate, Second World War veteran, and entrepreneur in the then fledgling field of information technology. In June 1970 he funded a display on Capitol grounds to "arouse public opinion in behalf of the release of American Prisoners of War" and encouraged tourists seeing it to demand their release. In *M.I.A. or Mythmaking in America*, Franklin described the display:

> At the center were the figures of two American prisoners. One sits in the corner of a bare cell, staring bleakly at an empty bowl and chopsticks on which a huge cockroach is perched. On the floor are other cockroaches and a large rat. The other figure lies in a bamboo cage, ankles shackled. By the end of the year, this tableau was being set up in state capitols throughout the country.[28]

Franklin's description of Perot's exhibit as "simulated imagery" was apt, because few if any POWs were held in the conditions it portrayed. Its effect on public perception was to demonize the Vietnamese and their communist leaders and to displace the war itself, the actual war, from American memory. Missing as well was any hint that some American prisoners had by then, 1970, turned against the war and developed empathy for the Vietnamese. By that time, the mythology of flyers shackled in bamboo cages was already being monetized by the Victory in Vietnam Association.

BRACELETS BY VIVA

The Victory in Vietnam Association, known as VIVA, was chartered in California in 1967 as a tax-exempt educational organization to counter the effectiveness of the antiwar movement. It changed its name to Voices in Vital America in 1969 and began to sell metal bracelets with the names of POWs and MIAs engraved. Soon, says Franklin, VIVA was wholesaling bracelets through the League, Ross Perot's People United We Stand organization, and Junior Chambers of Commerce across the country. The bracelets were a moneymaking bonanza:

Retailers kept 50 cents for each $2.50 nickel-plated bracelet and a dollar for each $3.00 copper bracelet, with the remaining two dollars going to VIVA whose costs averaged less than 50 cents per bracelet. . . . By early 1972, VIVA was distributing more than five thousand bracelets a day. . . . VIVA's income soared to $3,698,575 in 1972 and, despite the January 1973 peace accords, to $7,388,088 for 1973.[29]

Among the four to ten million Americans wearing the bracelets when the war ended were political figures Richard Nixon and George Wallace, actors Charlton Heston and Bill Cosby, the Dodgers' star pitcher Don Drysdale, and singers Johnny Cash and Sonny Bono.[30]

THE POW-MIA FLAG

The bracelets vaulted the POW-MIA issue to stratospheric emotional levels and lent political tonnage to the public's support of Nixon's pledge to keep the war going until "the last man comes home." But it was the POW-MIA flag designed and distributed by the National League of Families that became the most enduring symbol through which Americans came to remember the war in Vietnam. Flown over the White House on federal holidays every year since 1982, the flag shows a bowed black head with barbed wire strung beneath its chin with a guard tower looming in the background. The flag now flies daily above many state buildings across the country.

The Reagan administration throughout the 1980s maintained a *POW-MIA Fact Book* claiming "it would be impossible to rule out the possibility that live Americans are being held." The 1990 edition printed by the Bush administration said its POW-MIA efforts were "predicated on the assumption that some are still alive."[31]

The words "You are not forgotten," running across the bottom of the flag, disassociates those who fly the flag from those who would forget those left behind. It was a distinction that conjured weak-kneed Washington insiders who accepted Hanoi's denial that it was holding more prisoners than it admitted. The ending of the war on terms favorable to the North Vietnamese, said right-wing critics, confirmed that communist influence had penetrated the highest levels of national security—an echo of the Cold War conspiracism that had helped initiate the U.S. military mission to Southeast Asia in the first place. The soft-on-communism canard would remain a staple in the betrayal narrative for the loss of the war that would resound through America's end-of-century political culture.

ENEMIES: INSIDE THE BELTWAY AND THE WALLS OF HOA LO

American paranoia about communism goes back at least to the 1917 Bolshevik Revolution in Russia and the formation of the U.S. Communist Party in 1919. The CPUSA was instrumental in the rise of the CIO unions in the 1930s and a voice in early warnings of European fascism that kept it in the conservative crosshairs into the 1940s. Communism gained international stature through its role in the Second World War defeat of Nazi Germany, and communist-affiliated labor unions and political parties in Western Europe rode that popularity—and their own anti-fascist credentials—to new heights in the postwar years.[32]

Business and political leaders in the United States were unsettled enough by the Red tide arising abroad, but the specter of home-front communist influence was still more alarming. Fears that communist ideas were subverting religious and family values had the country on edge; speculation that communists had already infiltrated higher education and the entertainment industry set in motion efforts to purge the radicals. When suspicions arose of communists in the government, the country was overtaken by a mass hysteria that came to be known as McCarthyism.[33]

The communists were targeting the national security state, said Wisconsin senator Joseph McCarthy, and the bull's-eye was the Army itself. McCarthy's allegations led to the 1954 Army-McCarthy hearings during which the senator claimed to have a list of subversives in the State Department and the military. The hearings came at a time when emotions from the stalemated war in Korea were still settling and the country was grappling with rumors that some of its soldiers had crossed over to the communist North or Red China.

McCarthy's "list" never materialized, but the sensitivities raised by it carried over into the years of America's war in Vietnam. When GIs and veterans began coming out against the war and aligning themselves with left-wing organizations—said by rightists to be communist-front groups—Americans of various political stripes sensed a second coming of the McCarthy years. Post-1973 news that some POWs home from Hanoi had spoken out against the war while in lockup, combined with rumors that not all of the captured Americans had come home or were even accounted for, prolonged public curiosity about "what really went on over there." Dissenters among the returning captives, such as Wilber, Miller, and the Peace Committee, were now grist for imagining that they knew something about the missing and had even colluded with their communist jailers in the disappearance of their own comrades or, to give the conspiracy a twist, that they were colluding now with government insiders in a cover-up of the truth about the missing.

Privately funded POW-MIA rescue missions in the late 1970s came up empty-handed, as at Son Tay. Postmortems on the missions often pursued conspiratorial sell-out theories that led back to Washington—someone inside the Beltway had tipped off the communists that "we," the rescuers, were coming. By the early 1980s, films like *Uncommon Valor* were turning POW-MIA betrayal tales into box office gold.

JOHN McCAIN: ANOTHER MANCHURIAN CANDIDATE?

Although inspired by Hollywood, the most hardcore of the MIA betrayal tales emerged on the campaign trail. For a March 13, 2000, article in *Newsweek*, H. Ross Perot told the reporter that "he believes the senator [McCain] hushed up evidence that live POWs were left behind in Vietnam and even transferred to the Soviet Union for human experimentation, a charge Perot says he heard from a senior Vietnamese official in the 1980s." Perot added, "There's evidence,

evidence, evidence. . . . McCain was adamant about shutting down anything to do with recovering POWs."[34]

The story of POWs being traded to the Soviets had roots in Nelson Demille's 1988 novel *Charm School*, in which U.S. POWs have been traded to the Soviets. The Soviets are training Americans to be infiltrated back to the United States as agents. But were the traded Americans POWs or defectors? If defectors, at what point had they "gone over"? Years later, in Demille's story, the United States launches a raid. To rescue POWs? Or to assassinate defectors? The touch of nonfiction in the story's provenance is that Demille claimed in the book's preface that he had learned of pilots traded to the Soviets at Phu Bai airbase while stationed there during the war.

Two years later, freelance journalist Ted Sampley self-published his article, "John McCain: The Manchurian Candidate," claiming that Vietnamese communists tried to "turn American POWs into agents." Sampley cited the claim made by former Soviet KGB major Oleg Kalugin that "one of the POWs worked on by the KGB was a `high-ranking naval officer' who . . . agreed to work with the Soviets upon his repatriation to the United States and has frequently appeared on U.S. television." Sampley wrote that "Sen. John McCain fits [Kalugin's] description" and that the fact that he was a senator should not rule out the Manchurian Candidate possibility.

In June 1998, a stunning version of *Charm School* was broadcast on CNN as "Valley of Death," the product of months of investigative legwork. The report was that U.S. Special Forces had used Sarin nerve gas in "Operation Tailwind," a 1970 covert raid to assassinate a group of GIs who had defected to the North Vietnamese in Laos. Defected? Or were the targets really POWs that the U.S. government never wanted to come home? Had some of the war's MIAs actually been POWs that the government assassinated? The primetime broadcast, with legendary war reporter Peter Arnett narrating, only opened the question. A month later, CNN retracted the story and fired its producer, April Oliver.[35]

THE WAR IN VIETNAM FOR AMERICANS was very much about
the communist leadership of the Hanoi government in the North
and the National Liberation Front in the South. Although scholars
and some politicians knew communism to be a social and economic
system with features attractive to American workers—should they
know the truth about it—government and business leaders used their
power in religious and secular institutions to portray communism as
a belief system based on lies, its followers dupes, victims of deceit and
deception. Communism was godless, and Christian believers were
called to the war against it.

As a war against mendacity with a religious tonality, the U.S.
military campaign in Vietnam appealed to America's foundational
mission as the "city on a hill," a beacon of divine light for a world
vulnerable to the evils of the material world. The war had been a test
of faith and the lures of draft resistance—"Girls say yes to boys who
say no" went one antiwar slogan—dissent-in-uniform, and desertion, revealed the weaknesses of many young Americans. But the GIs,
Marines, sailors, and flyers who resisted those temptations and fought
the "good fight" came home with honor and went on to canonized
heroism in "the official story."

6

A Captive Nation: POWs as Grist for the American Myth

A people's narrative is the story they tell about themselves, the story of how and why they came to be what they believe they are. The American story braids together religious and secular themes for a story about the "good people" threatened by powers that could destroy the group from the outside and the weakness of those on the inside who might betray the group. The religious strands of that story are as old as Genesis where Eve is unable to resist the tree of knowledge forbidden to her by God. From the Garden of Eden onward, the plight of humankind is a series of God's tests that winnow the weak from the strong, the true believers from the pretenders to grace.

Many of God's tests involve deception. In the New Testament, God's people are fooled into following the false prophets of Antichrist, the Beast, because he masquerades as good and promises relief from earthly miseries. Antichrist is revealed in governments and social policies that promise peace, justice, security, and happiness, when, in fact, these goals are achievable only through loyalty to God, not government. According to the prophets, God obligates his people to discern good from bad among those seeking earthly power. As a project begun by Puritans in the seventeenth century, young America was lulled with images of its place in the biblical narrative.[1]

JOHN SMITH AND POCAHONTAS

The first literature produced by colonial America was the so-called captivity narrative, stories written by Americans about themselves or others who had been captured by Indians. In a 1999 study of that genre, anthropologist Pauline Turner Strong wrote that American identity took form through representations of "struggles in and against the wild: struggles of a collective Self surrounded by a threatening but enticing wilderness, a Self that seeks to domesticate this wilderness as well as the savagery within itself." John Smith's story is one of the classics of the tradition.

Smith was captured on a reconnaissance mission into Indian territory, December 1607, six months after the founding of Jamestown. His captors were warriors of the Pamunkey tribe, led by chief Powhatan. Smith was held for several weeks, during which time he was spared from death by Powhatan's lovestruck daughter, Pocahontas. Smith negotiated his release, receiving land for Jamestown in return for his promise of cannons and a grindstone for the Indians. By this account, Smith saved Jamestown. Smith was a hero.[2]

Smith's story became the basis for his lionization in American history, but subsequent interpretations of what really happened during his captivity render it the stuff of myth. Strong points out that, even in the sixteenth century, the saving of Europeans by native princesses was already a literary cliché; she goes on to suggest that when Pocahontas "saved" Smith by casting her body between his head and the Indians' clubs, she was actually playing a role in a rebirthing ritual designed to transform Smith into a Pamunkey. In short, says Strong, Smith was probably submitted to an adoption ceremony, not an execution.[3]

The mythical qualities in Smith's version of his capture lie in the ambiguity it created about the firmness of the psychosocial boundary

between him and the native Other who held him. In the anthropological light shed on his and stories like it, we're led to consider that
the captivity experience may have confronted him with his own inner
"savagery" and his vulnerability to Pamunkey paganism. Had Smith
conjured the story of his near execution in order to disguise, even to
himself, the appeal that conversion to "Indianism" had had on him?
And was the hint of Pocahontas's seductiveness in the rescue scene
a storytelling ploy to divert questions that might arise in Jamestown
about his own attraction to the unbridled (as the English saw it) sexu-
ality of the Indian girl and the impotence of the Puritan ethic as a
restraint on him in that situation?

These questions were only implicit in Smith's story, but they gained
prominence as new chapters were added to the captivity canon during
the Indian wars at the end of the century. The narrative of temptation,
punishment, and redemption that stories like Smith's framed became
more complex after several instances of captives, apparently giving
in to their inner Indian, rejecting the Puritan path and choosing to
remain with their erstwhile captors. Those stories, in the hands of
early eighteenth-century preachers, gave the captivity literature the
qualities it needed for a meaningful interface with the POW narrative
coming out of Vietnam some 350 years later.

KOREA, VIETNAM, AND THE RESUSCITATION OF AMERICA'S CAPTIVITY NARRATIVE

The captive Self and the captivating Other, as anthropologist Strong
puts it, are the oppositional poles between which American identity is
formed. That process of identity creation went on well into the nine-
teenth century as the ongoing conquest of North American Indians
reproduced the need of Americans to see goodness in themselves and
evil in others. The great and victorious wars of the twentieth century—the war to end all wars, 1917–1918, and the war against fascism,
1941–1945—did not tax that self-identity unduly, but the return of
U.S. expansionism in the post–Second World War years did. A crisis
of legitimacy that began with the war in Korea grew to dangerous

levels during the Vietnam war years, requiring nourishment for the
American images of Self and Other.

   As if scripted by history, those wars in Vietnam and Korea also
produced timely new generations of captives with stories that would
reinvigorate the nation's collective narrative. Perhaps because the war
in Vietnam followed so closely on the heels of Korea, it was the former
that would make the greater contribution to the captivity literature.
The facts of the war's widely perceived illegitimacy and its loss would,
however, cause that narrative to turn inward with an intensity it had
never had, spawning a search for the enemy within, and the imagining of that enemy in the absence of the real thing.

   The new chapter of the "captive America" narrative that the POW
experience of the Vietnam era would write, then, had, like the previous chapters, as much to say about America itself as its enemy.

GOOKS: THE ASIAN "OTHER" RACIALIZED

The representations of the POW experience in Southeast Asia did say
a great deal about the enemy, of course, and much of it followed in the
tradition of racial disparagement characteristic of the 300-year-old
captivity stories. By the time the war began, moreover, that tradition had been given a specifically Asian twist by the war against the
Japanese during the 1940s and the Korean War of the early 1950s. In
both those conflicts, U.S. propaganda depicted Asians with slanted
eyes, buck teeth, and sloping foreheads. In his book, *North Korea:
Another Country*, Bruce Cumings recalls Koreans being described
by *New York Times* military editor Hanson Baldwin as "barbarians,"
"primitive peoples," "armored horde," and "invading locusts." Other
U.S. leaders and publications called them "half-crazed automatons"
and "wildmen with arrested development." This "nauseating stew
of racial stereotypes," wrote Cumings, stirred diverse peoples into a
nameless sludge that accumulated under one name: "gook."[4]

   The term "gook" carried over from the Korean War, becoming the
appellation of choice for Americans referring to the Vietnamese. By
the late 1960s, GIs arriving in Vietnam were quickly introduced to

that word and its extended lexicon of "slants," "slopes," "zips," and "dinks" that diminished the people they were ostensibly there to support. Former POWs also adopted that language for their memoirs. In *Before Honor*, Eugene McDaniel describes one of his guards, measuring about five feet ten inches, as the world's tallest "gook"; about another he wrote, "savage, and that said it all." Larry Guarino wrote without apparent sarcasm that Vietnamese "brains functioned on different frequencies from ours . . . so I gave up any thought of reasoning with them and declared them to be 'just gooks.'" Ralph Gaither recalls being driven from Camp Dogpatch to Hanoi by "a bunch of gooks." [5]

Racist portrayals of the Vietnamese appear in most of the POW memoirs, and in some instances the writers use descriptions of deviant behavior and local customs to make their point. Gaither, for example, described what he saw from Dogpatch:

> The guards made horrible sport of butchering their food. When they killed a pig, they first punched its eyes out so that it would stand still, then they beat it to death. Cows suffered a like fate. They tied them with ropes strung all over like a spider web, and then beat them to death with an ax. The women killed the dogs for meat by hanging them in a grotesque position and then beat them with sticks. All the while the guards and women laughed as though they were at a sports event.

From that, he concluded, "You could not generate much respect for such people as that. We prisoners could not expect much better treatment than they gave their animals and that's about what we got." [6]

One may take at face value the accuracy of Gaither's report and still question his use of it to describe the treatment of POWs. Cruelty to animals might predict cruelty to people, but we would have to know more about the cultural practices of the people and circumstances surrounding the events he witnessed before accepting the analogy he constructs. Using the treatment of animals as an indicator for the national character entails an even greater leap. Even though U.S. treatment of prisoners was as bad or worse as that dished out by the

North Vietnamese, one could make little sense out of that record by having witnessed, say, U.S. soldiers shooting elephants from helicopters for sport. For that matter, Vietnamese prison guards are likely to have been a small and select portion of the population, from which, whatever their behavior, it would be dangerous to generalize about the nation's people.

THE CAPTIVE SELVES IN HOA LO PRISON

The enduring presence of the terrifying oriental Other in the Vietnam POW story is based less on America's continuing need to believe the worst about the Vietnamese than on the way that image helps construct what Americans want to think about themselves. Not only are "we" not like "them," our POWs proved that Americans would not forsake themselves or their nation even under the extreme conditions of imprisonment by the enemy. The standard account of the American POWs in this narrative is that the abrupt cessation of torture in late 1969 was due to the death of the devilish Ho Chi Minh, or to the early release of a few prisoners whose public testimony on torture upon return to the States sparked a letter-writing campaign by the POWs' families that put pressure on the Hanoi government to lighten up—an explanation supportive of the idea that the struggle of the prisoners, and their families by extension, was meaningful.[7] By this reasoning, the Vietnamese were a racial Other lacking the civilized sensibilities that peacenik naïveté imparted to them. Acceptance of this version, moreover, required belief that the prisoners were masters of their own fate, which made their improved conditions and eventual repatriation explainable as results of their own struggle, not of conciliation and peace.

But there is reason to wonder if the greatest change in 1969 was in Vietnamese prison practices or in the story told by the SROs about the pre-1969 conditions. Was it just a coincidence that conditions changed at Hoa Lo and other Northern camps at the same time the first large group of GIs captured in the South arrived there, or was their arrival the trigger for a change in the story the SROs needed to be told? Is it possible, in other words, that the disparity between the pre- and post-1969 conditions looks so great because the SROs constructed a kind of "bad ol' days" mythology that exaggerated the tough times they had been through in order to impress and establish authority over the newly arrived prisoners?

The suggestion of a political subtext to the SROs' story implies that there was a game of one-upmanship being played by the wannabe heroes who were sensitive to the weakness of their own credentials as tough-guy holdouts. The competing interpretations to be made of the rough interrogations that the captives were put through—was it torture in pursuit of militarily significant information or punishment for misconduct?—are still in play.

SELF-FLAGELLATED HEROES

The most fascinating renditions of the torture stories come from POWs who openly admit to having consciously provoked the Vietnamese to torture them, and at the time even inflicting physical injury on their own bodies, essentially torturing themselves when the Vietnamese wouldn't do it. Like Everett Alvarez, other pilots captured during the first year of the air war quickly recognized how little was at stake in the interrogation sessions and gave the Vietnamese useless information in order to avoid physical coercion. That changed, however, with the arrival in Hoa Lo of Navy Commander Jeremiah Denton.

Denton came in July of 1965 and declared himself in charge of the thirteen other captives, some of whom had been there for nearly a year. "Follow the Code," he ordered, and plan for escape and resistance. As it played out, Denton's order was a dangerous act of provocation by which, he admitted to the press years later, "We forced them to be brutal to us." There was a sadistic inflection in that approach, moreover, because Denton ordered all those POWs who had already "failed," by cooperating with the interrogators, to "bounce back" by confessing their weaknesses to him or another SRO and then return to interrogation sessions where they could then "succeed" in resistance and have another chance to endure torture. The threat for not repeating the cycle was that SROs might bring charges, years later after release, against the insubordinate underlings, who had been "broken" by the Vietnamese. Had that part of Denton's order been put into words for the press, it might have read, "We SROs forced the North Vietnamese to be brutal to our lower-ranking fellow POWs."[8]

James Stockdale and Robinson Risner followed Denton into the prison system a couple months later. For them, as for Denton, torture wasn't something to be avoided, but a test of will and faith to be passed. Reversing the conventional logic whereby torture was the consequence befalling the prisoner for failure to give the Vietnamese the information they wanted, the three leaders posited war as the normative relationship between the POWs and their captors, with torture being the form that combat took in those circumstances. For these hardliners, the cycle connecting interrogations and torture began with torture: to be "at torture" was the natural state-of-being for the American POW. Like any form of warfare, torture was painful, it took men to their limits, and required periodic retreats, that is, a return to the interrogations. But warriors bounce back, they return to combat, and the prisoner *at* war uses the interrogations as the road to take back to the front lines where he belongs—in the stocks, under the lash, and in the ropes.[9]

The fact that senior officers among the POWs actually provoked mistreatment by the Vietnamese has always been an asterisk on the torture stories that POWs told upon their return. But, as a segue to the religious subtext that makes the Vietnam-era POW stories so resonant with the early American captivity narrative, the accounts coming out of Hanoi of self-inflicted bodily pain are still more poignant. In January 1969, for example, Stockdale began fasting to protest Vietnamese attempts to extract what even he knew was useless five-year-old information from him about his unit. Then, fearing that they might try to film him for propaganda purposes, he battered his own face with a stool and cut his scalp to create wounds that would appear to have been inflicted by his captors. Stockdale's self-mutilation became a kind of theater that he staged in order to assuage his anxiety and self-doubt, with his most effective prop being the "puke balls" he made by swallowing soap and then vomiting. This abuse of himself went on for days, with self-delivered "early morning bashings" that turned his face and hands into mashed flesh. "It really became a test of self-discipline," he recalled later.[10]

Risner in his book told a similar story. Fearing he might be photographed or filmed for propaganda purposes, he said he first considered killing himself and then thought about cutting the tendons in his hands. He doesn't say what purpose crippled hands would have served in that context, leaving the reader to surmise that he added it to his story to conjure images of self-administered crucifixion. In any case, Risner eventually reasoned that it was his voice that the Vietnamese really wanted. Since he was a high-profile captive, an American hero even in the eyes of his fellow inmates, his voice heard reading news or information over Radio Hanoi would lend credibility to North Vietnamese broadcasts. So it was his voice that he would deny them.

Recalling that drinking acid or striking the throat could damage the voice, Risner knelt and prayed. "I said, 'Lord, is this the right way to go? Should I cut my wrists? Should I try to destroy my voice?'" With or without divine guidance (he doesn't say), Risner went for the throat:

> I began pounding my throat as hard as I could. My eyes watered and sometimes I saw stars. I gave frequent chops to the throat.... I choked and struggled to get my breath. My neck swelled up, but it did not affect my voice. I could still talk.

Risner turned to the acid treatment, counting on his soap to have enough lye in it to damage his throat:

> I took my cup and filled it with a third cup of water, and part of a bar of lye soap. I crumbled, mashed, and stirred it into a mushy, mucky substance. Then I began gargling with it. It burned the inside of my mouth like fire, almost cooking it, and I accidentally

swallowed some. The taste was enough to make me vomit. To increase the effect of the acid, I decided also to try to damage my vocal cords. I held a rag or towel over my mouth and screamed as loud as I could but at the same time compressing the air I was expelling so there would not be much noise. I continued this for three days and nights, staying awake as much as possible. By the third day, I could not whisper. I tried to talk, then tried to sing. I could not do either. It had worked! I was now a mute.

It didn't work, and Risner wasn't a mute; one good cough the next day and his voice was back, leaving him with nothing but diarrhea for his effort.[11]

For Denton, Stockdale, Risner, and other hardliners, torture became a way to confirm their worth as American warriors. Evidence of physical damage from torture, they hoped, would be evidence, upon their release, that they had remained *at* war during their imprisonment. When the torture they wanted from the Vietnamese wasn't forthcoming, they provoked it. When that didn't work, they inflicted their own damage. As Stockdale put it in his memoir, he prayed that his binge of self-flagellation would "make Syb [his wife, Sybil] and those boys of ours proud."[12]

The story of prisoners *at* war is the "official story," but it is the story of only a few of the hardcore SROs and it isn't always clear that the war being fought within Hoa Lo was the same war being fought outside the walls. It appears upon reexamination, for example, that SRO demands that prisoners resist interrogations had little to do with military strategy and a lot to do with SRO control over the prison population and the twisted sense of self-discipline for which some SROs like Stockdale needed to have validated by being tortured. Likewise, the resistance of senior officers to what they considered their exploitation for propaganda purposes probably had more to do with the war in America than the war in Vietnam. Robinson Risner's futile effort to disable his voice lest he be forced to read something over Radio Hanoi that the other POWs might hear is a case in point.[13]

Risner doesn't say what it was that he would have had to read, nor does he date the time of his struggle with that issue, but it occurred about the time of a similar incident described by Stockdale in his memoir. Stockdale objected to prisoners being used to "read the news" because he had learned in a course at Stanford University, "Comparative Marxist Thought," taught by "an old Kremlinologist who knew all [the Marxist strands], that the use of prisoners that way could be manipulated for brainwashing." The point had been driven home for Stockdale by tapes made by psychologists who had studied POWs from the Korean War.[14]

But is that what was going on in Hoa Lo? By Stockdale's own account—dismissed by him as communist trickery—the Vietnamese wanted an American to read the news because their interpreters did not have sufficient skill in English to be understood by the Americans. And what was the news they wanted read? Stockdale recalled it being *New York Times* excerpts from the paper's assistant managing editor Harrison Salisbury, who had recently returned from his fact-finding trip to Hanoi. True, Salisbury had come back to the United States critical of the Johnson administration's Vietnam policy, but if there was a credible source to be had from the U.S. side of the war, he was it.[15] Stockdale nevertheless put out an order that participation in the readings should stop, and twenty years later, in his memoirs, he stuck to the Cold War silliness that Salisbury's *Times* report was "loaded with what we had all been getting for months as the [Communist] Central Committee's propaganda line."[16]

Taken at face value, Stockdale's denial of the news to the POWs appears due to his fear that the ideological war beyond the walls of Hoa Lo was more than his men could handle. So it was best to protect them from it. Led by the reinterpretations of other captivity stories made by Strong and Gruner, however, we have to ask now if what Stockdale feared more was the enemy inside the walls, indeed the enemy within the hearts and minds of the POWs themselves.

The SROs' fear that their underlings might defect, and evidence for the legitimacy of that fear, can be found in the memoirs. By the early 1970s, there was open rebellion against the SRO leadership. As discussed in chapter 3, some of the discontent was fomented by the

newly arrived POWs from the South who had survived jungle confinement for months and years before arriving in the Hanoi system.
Their experience made them skeptical of SRO "authority" that was
based on the officers' claims to having suffered abuse between 1965
and 1969.[17]

THE POWs IN THE AMERICAN CAPTIVITY NARRATIVE

There was more to antiwar dissent than struggle over the distribution
of power among the inmates, but that issue is a clue to understanding
the Vietnam-era prisoner experience as an extension of the American
captivity narrative. The resistance of rank-and-file POWs and dissident officer-pilots like Wilber and Miller to the control of the SROs,
who were committed to their own place in a post-release hero-prisoner script, was accompanied by emotional sentiments that aligned
them with the Vietnamese, the enemy Other as seen by hardliners.

It was the humanizing of the Other that the SROs feared because
recognition of the humanity in "them" meant recognizing an element
of them in "us," an acknowledgment of the enemy within the hearts
and minds of GIs, of Marines, of fellow pilots.

With the abundant inconsistencies in the accounts of torture
handed out by the historians John Hubbell, Stuart Rochester, and
John Kiley, and the numerous references in the POW memoirs to
SRO fears of the "white gook" within themselves or their comrades,
it seems likely that, as much as for John Smith, it was the *attraction* of
the Other that scared the SROs. It was enough to mask their vulnerability with a counternarrative about the terror that the Vietnamese
visited upon them. In short, it's possible that it wasn't the extinguish-
ing of themselves they feared—execution in the Smithian legend—so
much as their conversion to the ways of the Vietnamese and the righ-
teousness of their cause.

Reflecting on his own interrogation experience, Army captain John
Dunn turned over the same stone that obscured the Pamunkey side
of history for centuries when he wrote that his prison administrator
"seemed more interested in conversion than . . . the application of

torture to obtain information." Dunn's insight wasn't just imaginative. Many of the POWs described the education programs the Vietnamese provided for them, the content of which seems to have differed little from what was being taught in U.S. college classrooms by the late 1960s: the history of Vietnamese struggles for independence, the details of the Geneva Accords that had ended the French occupation and artificially divided the country, and basic political economy. From what we know, there was little in the Hoa Lo "lesson plans" for POWs that is not today the accepted wisdom of what the war was about. That being the case, the claim by one of the Vietnamese interrogators that the prisoners were being given "the right to rebirth," seems all the more plausible, all the more sincere, all the more resonant with take-two on the John Smith legend.[18]

7

The Heritage of Conscience: From the American War in Vietnam to America Today

The in-service resistance carried out during the war in Vietnam by airmen, Marines, GIs, and sailors was documented by David Cortright in his 1975 book *Soldiers in Revolt* and brought to the screen in 2006 in David Zeiger's film *Sir! No Sir!* Cortright and Zeiger's contributions to American history and public memory of the war are, however, exceptions in the volumes of scholarly work and popular culture with which most Americans are familiar. All too often, those better-known accounts leave out the story that some of the warriors sent to fight the war also fought gallantly against it. The fact that POWs held in Hanoi numbered among those dissenters has been all but erased from the record.

CARRYING IT ON

The heritage of service members and veterans who acted with conscience to help end the war in Vietnam was kept alive in the decades that followed by the men and women who had formed Vietnam Veterans Against the War (VVAW). Throughout the 1980s, VVAW rallied against U.S. interventions in Central America, often forming the lead contingents for protest marches in Washington, D.C., and New York City. And individual veterans, who may or may not have been members of VVAW, provided some of the most powerful profiles of service members' lifelong commitments to peace and postwar reconciliation.

CHARLIE CLEMENTS

Charlie Clements graduated second in his class at the Air Force Academy and flew missions in Vietnam before citing moral grounds in refusing to fly anymore. Remanded to a military hospital for psychiatric evaluation, he left the military, became a doctor, and inspired a new generation of activists working to end American wars abroad. His book and Oscar-winning 1986 film *Witness to War* documented the indigenous resistance to the U.S. puppet regime in El Salvador and made known to a broader public the work done by Medical Aid to El Salvador, an organization he helped found.

JAN BARRY

Sent to Vietnam in 1962 as a radio technician, Jan Barry felt an immediate connection with the Vietnamese who worked on his base in Nha Trang. Appointed to West Point upon returning stateside, he grew increasingly unhappy with the war, and dropped out after the U.S. launched air strikes against North Vietnam in 1964. Barry joined the Spring Mobilization to End the War in Vietnam in April 1967 and in June helped draft the bylaws for Vietnam Veterans Against the War. Today, Barry is an acclaimed poet, considered by writer and critic W. D. Ehrhart to be "the most important figure" in the Vietnam generation of poets.

CHUCK SEARCY

Searcy was an intelligence analyst based near Saigon in 1966. The information he gathered led him to question the truth of what the government was telling the American people about the war. Upon return, he graduated from the University of Georgia and edited a newspaper in Athens, Georgia. In 1992 he returned to Vietnam to help locate and defuse unexploded bombs dropped by the United States that continued to kill and maim Vietnamese farmers. After international acclaim for his work with Project Renew, an effort to locate and disarm unexploded ordnance in Quang Ngai Province, Searcy, now in his seventies, continues his mission of peace.[1]

SUSAN SCHNALL

After graduation from Stanford University's nursing program in 1967 and commissioning as a U.S. Navy officer, Susan Schnall was sent to Oak Knoll Naval Hospital in Oakland, California, where she took care of casualties from Vietnam. Made aware of a GI and veterans march for peace in the San Francisco Bay Area in October 1968, she got involved and organized her corpsmen and WAVEs to participate. They put up posters in the hospital at night that were torn down by the morning. Thinking she could do more, she contacted a friend who was a pilot, filled his single-engine plane with fliers about the upcoming demonstration, and dumped them from the air over five military installations in the San Francisco Bay Area. On October 12, Lieutenant Junior Grade Schnall participated in a demonstration in her uniform for which she was court-martialed.

When charges were dismissed, Schnall moved to New York to do clinical work and organize for health care reform, including, at the time, Medical Aid for Indochina, which raised money for medical supplies that went to the North and the National Liberation Front. Since 2006 she has led efforts to aid Vietnamese victims of Agent Orange, and she also works with Veterans for Peace (VFP). Reflecting on her life of activism for an August 22, 2019, interview, Schnall mused on the importance of people knowing they can take a step against authority and say, "I disagree with you, and I'm going to do something about it." And by doing that "you'll survive with your moral conscience intact."[2]

THE HERITAGE ORGANIZED:
VIETNAM VETERANS AGAINST THE WAR TO IRAQ
VETERANS AGAINST THE WAR

The spirit of peace born in Vietnam carried into the twenty-first century. Following the invasion of Iraq in the spring of 2003, a new generation of veterans attending the 2004 VFP annual convention formed Iraq Veterans Against the War (IVAW) with VVAW as an organizational model. In March 2008, IVAW conducted hearings that exposed atrocities committed or witnessed by its members in Iraq, a whistle-blowing exercise modeled after VVAW's Winter Soldier hearing in 1971.[3]

The organized expressions of dissent manifesting as IVAW is the most significant legacy of the Vietnam generation's dissent. But it is easy to imagine that others, inspired by their dissenting forebears and acting as individuals, stepped up to protest the new wars in the Middle East. Matthew Hoh, Ann Wright, and Pat Tillman were among them.

MATTHEW HOH

Matthew Hoh took part in the American occupation of Iraq in 2004–5 with a State Department reconstruction and governance team, and then in 2006–7 in Anbar Province as a Marine Corps company commander. On State Department assignment in 2009, Hoh resigned in protest of the Obama administration's escalation of the war against the Taliban. In 2010 he was awarded the Ridenhour Prize Recipient for Truth Telling named for Ron Ridenhour, the Vietnam veteran who exposed the 1968 My Lai Massacre. Today, Hoh is on the boards of Veterans for Peace and World Beyond War and is a frequent contributor to American news media. He has been a source for the *Washington Post* and *Wall Street Journal* and has been a guest on many network and cable television news programs.

ANN WRIGHT

Ann Wright retired as a colonel after thirteen years in the Army and sixteen years in the Army Reserves. She went to work for the U.S. State Department Foreign Service in 1987 and facilitated the opening of the U.S. Embassy in Afghanistan after the 2001 invasion of Afghanistan. Wright resigned in protest from the State Department the day before the 2003 invasion of Iraq. Wright has been arrested many times for protests of U.S. occupations in the Middle East and was one of three witnesses called to testify in June 2006 in support of U.S. Army Second Lieutenant Ehren Watada, who refused to deploy to Iraq with his unit, asserting that the war there violated the U.S. Constitution and international law.

PAT TILLMAN

Pat Tillman was a standout linebacker at Arizona State University, picked in the football draft in 1998 by the Arizona Cardinals. Profoundly moved by the attacks of September 11, 2001, he turned down a three-year contract worth $3.6 million and enlisted in the Army. In spring 2003, he deployed for the invasion of Iraq, disappointed to not be sent to Afghanistan in pursuit of the alleged 9/11 perpetrator, Osama bin Laden.[4]

The apparent conflation of U.S. leaders' missions in Iraq and Afghanistan was Tillman's first inkling that there was more to the American agenda in the Middle East than met the eye. Tillman's biographer Jon Krakauer, with access to Tillman's personal journal, noted his disillusionment with the war in Iraq. In words echoing Vietnam War POW dissidents James Daly or Bob Chenoweth, Tillman had written: "You know, some of these [Iraqi] kids are getting to me. . . . There are some very good people, especially some of these kids." With time, his feelings against the war would harden.

By May 2003, Tillman was complaining about leaders "telling guys to shoot innocent people only to be ignored by privates with cooler heads." By the time he redeployed to Afghanistan, he had become interested in Noam Chomsky's ideas and was looking forward to a meeting with the professor when he returned home.[5]

On April 22, 2004, Tillman was killed in a friendly fire incident. Evidence that the deadly rounds were fired within ten yards of him, and revelations that his uniform and his recent journal with his thoughts about the war had been burned at Forward Operating Base Salerno from which his unit worked, spawned rumors that he had been assassinated. Krakauer later dismissed the assassination idea as conspiratorial speculation.[6]

THE BLOWBACK TO CONSCIENCE

If the heritage of the conscientious rejection of war exercised by the Vietnam generation of GIs, POWs, and veterans reemerged in the biographies of Ann Wright, Matthew Hoh, Pat Tillman, and the veterans who organized IVAW, it would be an inspiring story certain to rouse the passions of war resisters going forward. But, as with the Newtonian principle that every action comes with an equal and opposite reaction, the steps taken toward peace by the dissidents locked in Hoa Lo and conscientious peers on the outside called forth the reaction of authorities and rejection by a Cold War–fearing public. Out of that push-and-pull, the betrayal narrative for the loss of the war forged discourses for political and ideological struggle over the U.S.'s twenty-first-century role in the world.

Units deployed to the Middle East were made up of volunteers, many of whom were hot to avenge the attacks of September 11, 2001. They arrived at Ayn al Asad Airbase in Iraq or Camp Phoenix in Kabul without the edges carried by draftees to Vietnam; military contracts with Burger King and other chains had homestyle comforts waiting for them.[7] Co-opted though they may have been by the relative comforts of new-century warfare, the ages of the troops—twenty-six was the mean age of the Americans killed in Iraq—and the educational backgrounds of many, like Pat Tillman, predisposed them to skepticism about the mission and its leaders once they saw it for real.

DISSENT PATHOLOGIZED AND MEDICALIZED:
"VICTIM-VETERANS" RE-UPPED

Simultaneous with the nudge toward resistance given by Hoh, Wright, and the IVAW leaders by the examples set by VVAW, dissent was discouraged and discredited.[8] Indeed, the coming-home story of the Iraq War veterans had been scripted before they left home. The dispatch of troops to the Persian Gulf in the fall of 1990 had drawn opposition from the antiwar movement. Prowar conservatives tried to discredit the movement by claiming it involved the same people who had spat on Vietnam veterans and betrayed the American mission in Southeast Asia. The Yellow Ribbon Campaign followed, and when troops returned in the spring of 1991, the news media lit up with reports of traumatized returnees returning to a public disinterested in their welfare.

The victim-veteran imagery—a carryover from the war in Vietnam—was tagged twelve years later by writers looking for ways to narrativize the new war. Joseph B. Verrengia, an Associated Press science reporter, prototyped the model that would shape news coverage of Iraq War veterans for years to come: "How many soldiers will require mental health treatment?" he asked in an April 18, 2003, story. Traumatized soldiers, he continued, "relive their horrors through flashbacks and nightmares, often followed by depression and fury." Moreover, he wrote, "this war [in Iraq] is colored by controversy and protests."[9]

Virtually every major newspaper would produce a feature story on "wounded warriors," many of them focused on the mental and emotional damage of the war. One of the earliest and most powerful was the *Boston Globe*'s four-part series, "The War After the War," begun in October 2006.[10]

The victim-veteran discourse so dominated the news of homecomings that dissent was squeezed out of the conversation. Thomas

Barton told Jerry Lembcke that when IVAW organizers visited New London, Connecticut, in 2006, the public's preoccupation with PTSD had made it harder to organize. "Everywhere we go," he said, "all people want to talk about is PTSD." The identity of veterans empowered and politicized by their wartime experience seemed overwritten by that of men and women home with unseen hurts asking for sympathy more than solidarity.[11]

DISSENT ABOARD THE CARRIER
USS *THEODORE ROOSEVELT*

As much as the conscientious dissent of the Vietnam-generation fighters and veterans played out in the new wars of the twenty-first century, it was met by an opposing reaction that also was descended, and inherited, from the same era. Indeed, the rise of the Trump movement in the early twenty-first century can best be understood as an extension of the betrayal narrative for the loss of the war in Vietnam. The Trump slogan, Make America Great Again (MAGA), posits a largely mythical prelapsarian America whose greatness was eroded by the permissiveness and economic entitlement programs associated with the 1960s.

But maybe that polarization is but a new beginning. The same push and pull, viewed by the German philosopher Hegel, is a *creative* energy leading not to a renewed stasis but a new, and higher, level of struggle. During the 2020 coronavirus pandemic, the virus broke out onboard the deployed aircraft carrier USS *Theodore Roosevelt*. The ship's captain, Brett Crozier, called for help from his chain of command in combatting the spread of the deadly virus among his crew. When his pleas went unheeded, he put the welfare of his sailors ahead of his own career and went around the usual channels with a letter to still higher ranks—an exercise of conscience befitting the dissident POW officers who sacrificed their careers to help end a war that was taking the lives of fellow fliers and shipmates.[12]

President Trump made known his displeasure with the captain, and on April 2, acting Navy secretary Thomas B. Modly fired Crozier.[13]

We don't know if the examples of Gene Wilber and Ed Miller were influences on Crozier. Cultural influence is elusive, intangible, touching the emotions as well as the mind. Maybe he encountered the history of the Hanoi dissenters in a class at the Academy, or maybe he just heard about it from classmates. Or maybe he saw *The Hanoi Hilton* movie. We don't know. Historians, in any case, make a distinction between objective and subjective social forces. It is a distinction that makes it less important that Crozier was moved by knowing that the officers held in Hanoi broke Navy protocol, resisted self-appointed authority figures, and stuck to their consciences. Maybe he was moved by something in his own background, social relations on board the carrier, and the organizational and political cultures of the times, as he saw them—objective social forces. We don't know.

The temptation to put Crozier's act of conscience on a trajectory tracing back to Hanoi grows stronger, however, when we see the same character displayed by his crew members. When Crozier departed *Theodore Roosevelt* after being fired, the crew gathered for a supportive mass farewell, chanting his name in respect, a rejection of the authorities who had cashiered the skipper for putting their well-being ahead of his own. A few days after Modly fired Crozier, he flew halfway around the world from inside the beltway, boarding the *Roosevelt* to justify his decision to the crew. Over the ship's intercom, Modly asserted that the captain had been canned because he was "stupid and naïve," to the apparent astonishment and ire of the crew. A recording of Modly's rant against Crozier taken from a loudspeaker in one of the many crew spaces also captures comments by listening sailors: "What the fuck?" "He was only trying to help us!" "Oh?" along with other muttered groans questioning Modly's characterization of this matter of courage and conscience.

Still, the conscientious actions in the Crozier affair and the crew's reaction could be an anomaly, an exception to military obeisance to authoritarian political figures. An example is the pre–Second World War German military that fell in lockstep with the Hitler cult for a fascist crusade to restore German greatness allegedly lost in the First World War. It is that pattern in the historical record that unsettles some observers of the United States today. Might the threads of white supremacy and nationalism in the MAGA movement have been vested by Trump with the martial might to wrench American lost-war angst into something as dangerous as Germany's interwar revanchism?[14]

Ironically, the kind of servile military leadership that Trump had in mind might itself have been a casualty of the war in Vietnam. The May 18, 2020, The *New York Times* reported findings of a *Military Times* survey that "50 percent of active-service military hold an unfavorable view of the president." The *Times* quoted reporter Mark Bowden saying, "I have never heard officers in high positions express such alarm about a president," and called the Trump presidency a "slow-motion train wreck in civil-military relations."[15]

Fifty years after the war in Vietnam, the acts of conscience displayed there, and the reaction they provoked, continue to drive American political culture. The struggle over the heritage of that experience, waged between those who tell, interpret, and decide the uses to which it is put, looms as large as ever in the meaning of the war in the nation's present.

Notes

Introduction
1. In his essay, "Missing in Action in the 21st Century," H. Bruce Franklin outlines how Perot's Christmas package trip fit into the overall "Go Public Campaign" begun by the Nixon administration in March 1969 to stall the peace negotiations with the POW issue, https://www.hbrucefranklin.com/articles/missing-in-action-in-the-21st-century/.
2. Mary Hershberger, *Traveling to Vietnam: American Peace Activists and the War* (Syracuse, NY: Syracuse University Press, 1998), 177–200, has a detailed account of the Committee of Liaison's mail service.

1. Forgotten Voices from Hoa Lo Prison
1. The Code of Conduct (Article III) refers to "parole" and "special favors" as examples of things that a prisoner should not accept from their captors. Vietnam POW literature refers to a prisoner's acceptance of early release, or amnesty, as a violation of this article. Better food or medical care than given to their peers (interpreted as special favors) would be a similar violation.
2. The validity of the torture allegations will be explored in the following chapters. Relatedly, there are questions about the motivations for the harsh treatment, whatever its measure, that was meted out by the prison staff: was it punishment for breaking prison rules, a "brainwashing" tactic, or an effort to extract militarily sensitive information? According to historian John G. Hubbell in *P.O.W.: A Definitive History of the American Prisoner-of-War Experience in Vietnam, 1964–1973* (New York: Reader's Digest Press, 1976), Navy pilot James Stockdale,

shot down in September 1965, was still being tortured in 1969 for information on aircraft air defenses, which is unlikely since any information
obtained would have been outdated and useless to the Vietnamese
(476).

3.   Now used by establishment scholars to valorize its quality and legiti-
macy, and sardonically by critics, "official story," according to Stuart
Rochester and Frederick Kiley in *Honor Bound: American Prisoners
of War in Southeast Asia, 1961–1973* (Annapolis, MD: Naval Institute
Press, 1999), xi, was coined by English Professor Craig Howes in his
Voices of the Vietnam POWs: Witnesses to Their Fight (New York:
Oxford University Press), 75.

4.   Hubbell's *P.O.W.* acknowledgments give thanks to *Reader's Digest* edi-
tors Andrew Jones and Kenneth Y. Tomlinson for their help with the
research. Tomlinson's Wikipedia entry details his right-wing ties with
the Reagan and Bush presidencies and charges made against him for
the "propagandistic" quality of his work in the media. The Wikipedia
entry credits him with co-authorship of *P.O.W.*, while another site
credits Hubbell, Jones, and Tomlinson as authors.

5.   The Son Tay fiasco brings to mind *Team America*, a 2004 parody of
the U.S military's global operations. Produced by the creators of *South
Park*, the film portrays U.S. missions as hapless affairs, most of which
end in comical failure leaving conditions worse than they found them.

6.   See the *Politico.com* story on the exchange: https://www.politico.com/
story/2015/07/trump-attacks-mccain-i-like-people-who-werent-
captured-120317. See also Felicia Sonnez, "Donald Trump on John
McCain in 1999: 'Does being captured make you a hero?,'" *Washington
Post*, August 7, 2018.

7.   Howes, *Voices of the Vietnam POWs*, 234. Scott Blakey, *Prisoner at
War: The Survival of Commander Richard A. Stratton* (Garden City, NY:
Anchor Press, 1978), points to a class argument (205).

8.   Hubbell, *P.O.W.*, 75.

9.   The preoccupation of Americans with communist brainwashing is
evinced in its unlikely appearances. Carol McEldowney in *Hanoi
Journal, 1967* (Amherst: University of Massachusetts Press, 2007)
recounts going to Hanoi in 1967 with a delegation of U.S. peace activists. She saw and heard things that brought into question Washington's
version of events. In the journal she kept, she wondered on October 5
how she would be able to report on the trip "without seeming brainwashed" (58).

10. The details of Knutson's capture are from Hubbell, *P.O.W.*, 91. Many
POWs remember the anger of villagers directed at them but, contra
Knutson's story that villagers were "egged on by an officer," others say
that regular Army personnel protected them from the villagers. Bob
Fant recalls (interview with Tom Wilber, March 15, 2015) a soldier

standing with a rifle at "port arms" position defending Fant from
approaching locals. Some, like Frank Anton in *Why Didn't You Get Me
Out? Betrayal in the Viet Cong Death Camps; The Truth about Heroes,
Traitors, and Those Left Behind* (Arlington, TX: Summit, 1997), recall
villagers' acts of kindness (32).

11.   The battering of Knutson as described by Hubbell, in addition to the
injuries he suffered in the shootdown and the absence of any medical
attention, make remarkable Hubbell's report that by October 29 he was
already recovering. Hubbell, *P.O.W.*, 116.

12.   Ibid., 98.

13.   Hubbell's description of Alvarez's expectations that he will be hung by
his ankles, skinned, castrated, and decapitated are intriguing. There
is no footnote for that description, which leads us to wonder: is this
Hubbell's imagination at work or Alvarez's? In either case, it reads as a
deprecation of the Asian Other, born of Occidentalist prejudices. Used
uncritically, as it is by Hubbell, the words function as stage-setting for
the prisoner-at-war narrative the Hubbell is constructing. Hubbell,
P.O.W., 7.

14.   Interview by Tom Wilber, April 4, 2017, in Hanoi with Nguyen Minh
Y, retired army officer, who, as a junior officer, worked in the deten-
tion camps from the internment of Alvarez at Hoa Lo until calling off
the names one-by-one at the release of the last group of prisoners at
Gia Lam airport. See also Malcolm W. Browne, "Thousands Watch 67
Prisoners Depart," *New York Times*, March 30, 1973.

15.   Hubbell, *P.O.W.*, 118.

16.   Note the careful wording in Knutson's solely witnessed Silver Star
citation: "For gallantry and intrepidity in action against the enemy in
North Vietnam on 17 October 1965. Shortly after parachuting onto
enemy soil, he was surrounded by village militia armed with rifles. In
the face of great personal risk, he elected to fight rather than surrender.
Defending himself with his *service revolver, he shot at his rifle-armed
adversaries, inflicting two casualties* prior to being overwhelmed by
their superior numbers. By his daring actions, extraordinary courage,
and aggressiveness in the face of the enemy, he reflected great credit
upon himself and upheld the highest traditions of the Naval Service
and the United States Armed Forces" (italics added). The revolver he
carried was not a true "service revolver" in the sense of a weapon but
was issued and loaded as a search-and-rescue signaling device.

17.   Knutson admitted the illegality of the shooting in an interview with
Darrel Ehrlick for the Billings, Montana *Gazette*, November 11, 2015,

18.   As a result of Tom Wilber's inquiries seeking documentation in the
detention camp system, retired Hoa Lo staff helped locate in 2018 several caches of more than 100 copies of antiwar newspapers, including
GI-published titles such as *GI Press Service, The Bond, EPF Newsletter*,

Resistance, War Bulletin, The Second Front Review, YLO, Liberation News Service, Fort Lewis Free Press, which are in the process of being catalogued into the collection at Hoa Lo Prison Museum. These are actual papers made available to prisoners, some dated as early as 1968.

19. Hubbell, *P.O.W.*, 262.

20. Rochester and Kiley, *Honor Bound*, write, "Prisoners were aware of the Russell inquest and . . . the death of Norman Morrison" (193).

21. McEldowney, *Hanoi Journal*, 97.

22. Rochester and Kiley, *Honor Bound*, 442.

23. Mary Hershberger, *Traveling to Vietnam*, 23.

24. James Clinton, *The Loyal Opposition: Americans in North Vietnam, 1965–1972* (Niwot, CO: University of Colorado Press), 10. A delegation from the United States, Women's Strike for Peace, also went in the summer of 1965 but did not meet POWs at that time.

25. Staughton Lynd and Tom Hayden, *The Other Side* (New York: New American Library, 1966), 100.

26. Clinton, *The Loyal Opposition*, 18. Aptheker does not name the POWs they met.

27. Hubbell, *P.O.W.*, 438.

28. Nguyen Minh Y, one of the few English-speaking NLF officers in the prisons, and assigned to Hoa Lo from the arrival of the first prisoner, Alvarez, said that many pilots gave interviews and recorded statements purely as a way to let their families know that they were well treated. Mr. Y reflected that it was Nixon's fabrication of the POW treatment issue that caused POWs to be concerned about their families suffering from unfounded worries. Interview with Tom Wilber, Hanoi, May 6, 2019.

29. Hubbell, *P.O.W.*, 549. There are no footnotes in the book so we can't tell how he arrived at those numbers.

30. George Coker as quoted in Barbara Powers Wyatt, ed., *We Came Home* (Toluca Lake, CA: P.O.W. Publications, 1977).

31. Tom Wilber interview with Nguyen Minh Y, Hanoi, April 4, 2017. We discussed in detail the case of David Wesley Hoffman, his interview with George Wald where he detailed his medical care for his compound broken arm, his lengthy monologue filmed by interviewers from Medical Aid to Indochina in May 1972 criticizing the massive escalation of bombing, his participation among interviewees of Jane Fonda, his report of his good medical care immediately on his return, and the sudden reversal in his narrative upon his return to the United States. Mr. Y attributes this to opportunism and understands that returning prisoners needed to say what they needed to in order to reintegrate into their culture and careers and get on with their lives. In an interview on May 16, 2016, in his home in Haiphong, Tran Trong Duyet told Tom Wilber that the importance to him personally of ensuring that

prisoners were treated fairly was his respect for family. He relayed the grief felt in his family when the French came to his home in 1951, took his older brother outside and beheaded him. He did not want families of prisoners to worry or grieve.

32. McEldowney, *Hanoi Journal, 1967*, 100.

33. The HBO documentary *Jane Fonda in Five Acts* has video of Hoffman describing this after his release: "If Miss Fonda thinks for a moment that any of the people that she saw were able to speak freely she's got another thing coming . . . I think coerced is a very mild word. I've used the word 'torture' initially." Note that Hoffman is not claiming he was tortured, but that he used the word. Hoffman was shot down late in 1971 and torture was reported to have ended in 1969. Fonda: "I think they're lying and I think they're not only going to have to live with the fact that they were carrying out acts of murder for the rest of their lives, they're also going to have to live with the fact that they are lying." See also Vanderbilt Television News Archive, https://tvnews.vanderbilt. edu, *CBS News*, Friday, April 13, 1973, record number 228071.

34. Hubbell, *P.O.W.*, 576.

35. James Daly and Lee Bergman, *Black Prisoner of War: A Black Conscientious Objector's Vietnam Memoir* (Lawrence: University Press of Kansas, 2000), 190.

36. Anton, *Why Didn't You Get Me Out?*, 32.

37. Howes, *Voices of the Vietnam POWs*, 218. Our use of "Other" is in the anthropological sense of the term.

38. "Now, Mayhew judges the US aggression unjust. He says, moreover, on the radio and in the papers that his compatriots condemn it more and more vigorously. Two American women that he met in Hanoi confirmed this information, and moreover, he saw films on Moratorium Day in November 1969, in the United States." Theo Ronco, "How American Pilots Captured in North Vietnam Live," *L'Humanité*, November 5, 1970.

39. British journalist Felix Greene was one of the first Western reporters to cover the war from Vietnam. His *Vietnam! Vietnam!* (Palo Alto, CA: Fulton Publshing Company, 1966) was made available to prisoners by the wardens. Carrigan's reference to stateside prisons was his recognition that, after the war, he could be court-martialed and jailed for what he had said. See McEldowney, *Hanoi Journal, 1967*, 96–97.

2. Profiles of Dissent: Senior Officers

1. The minimum accepted IQ score for admission to Mensa International, sometimes called the "genius society," is 132 on the Stanford-Binet test and 148 on the Cattell test.

2. Miller responds to interviewers regarding his military career: Edison W. Miller Collection, (AFC/2001/001/33509), Veterans History Project,

American Folklife Center, Library of Congress, https://memory.loc.gov/diglib/vhp/story/loc.natlib.afc2001001.33509/

3. Wilber tells all of this in an oral history video held in the Walter Eugene Wilber Collection, AFC/2001/001/69160, Veterans History Project, American Folklife Center, Library of Congress, http://memory.loc.gov/diglib/vhp/bib/69160.

4. Wilber and Miller established their combat bona fides in the air over Korea, whereas neither Stockdale nor Denton flew in combat in Korea—somehow, they missed that. That they were hostile to Wilber and Miller is fact; efforts to account for that hostility should consider that the accomplishments of the latter amplified their own feelings of inadequacy.

5. In the movie *The Fog of War: Eleven Lessons from the life of Robert S. McNamara*, McNamara provides this explanation for the nature of his departure: "And I said to a very close and dear friend of mine, Kay Graham, the former publisher of the *Washington Post*, 'Even to this day, Kay, I don't know whether I quit or was fired.' She said, 'You're out of your mind. Of course you were fired.'"

6. Michael O'Connor, *MiG Killers of Yankee Station* (Friendship, WI: New Past Press, 2003), gives details how Wilber, after being ordered by air control to shoot down a MiG and then locked on to his target, was suddenly ordered by the air war commander to abort and depart the area. Wilber turned away from the MiG to return to the ship and another, undetected MiG shot him from behind (126–28).

7. In an interview on May 5, 2019, with Tom Wilber, former Hoa Lo prison supervisor Nguyen Minh Y used the term "single room" to describe how Wilber was housed at Hoa Lo. When questioned about the term "solitary confinement," Mr. Y was not in full agreement with the use of the term. He described the solo nature of solitary as having to do with the number of people in a room and that the prisoner was allowed to leave the room daily for bathing and meals and getting some exercise. To Mr. Y, coupling "solitary" with "confinement" would connote never being able to leave the cell, which, he said, was not the case. He stated that, in their opinion, having the privacy of living in a small room was more favorable and that it afforded more protection. He said that although the North Vietnamese Army eventually gained control of the Hoa Lo facility from the Hanoi police, they initially leased only "four or five rooms" for captured pilots, Lieutenant Junior Grade Alvarez being the first in August 1964. It was only when those first few rooms were full of single occupants and newly captured pilots arrived that the staff began to double up the prisoners. When the French controlled the prison, the population density of Hoa Lo was about four to five times the U.S. prisoner population density.

8. Ralph Gaither, *With God in a P.O.W. Camp* (Nashville, TN: Boardman Press, 1973), 26.

9.   Quoting POW memoirs, Hubbell and Rochester and Kiley use a mix of "cell" and "room" when referring to the holding facilities. Wilber's later interview was with Mike Wallace for CBS's *60 Minutes* after his release and return on April 1, 1973.

10.   In a May 6, 2019, interview with Tom Wilber, Nguyen Minh Y pointed out that the DRV did not build prison facilities for the pilots. The army gradually took over Hoa Lo prisons from the Hanoi police. Other than Hoa Lo, the facilities were not designed as prisons but were repurposed as such. For example, the Zoo site was selected because it was a compound for filmmaking built by the French that included kitchen and worker housing and a secure wall and gates to protect from theft.

11.   Gerald Coffee, *Beyond Survival: Building on Hard Times—A POW's Inspiring Story* (Aiea, Hawaii: Coffee Enterprises, Inc., 2013), 240.

12.   A copy of the transcript is in the author's possession. The portions used here have been edited for length and clarity only.

13.   Tom Wilber received a greeting from his father on his fifteenth birthday, June 19, 1970:

> Announcer: Here is the birthday message to his son from Walter Eugene Wilber, Commander, U.S. Navy, American pilot captured in the Democratic Republic of Vietnam.
> Wilber:
>> To: Mister Thomas Eugene Wilber, 3212 Edinburgh Drive, Virginia Beach, Virginia 23452, U.S.A.
>> From: Walter Eugene Wilber, Commander, U.S. Navy, Camp of Detention for US Pilots Captured in the Democratic Republic of Vietnam.
>> Dear Thomas, happy birthday! I hope June nineteenth will be a very happy day, Tom. I wish you the very best of health and happiness, and wish, too, that I could be with you on your fifteenth birthday, however, I send you lots of love from my heart. . . .
>> Have a happy summer vacation but remember to be safe. I know you, and your brothers and sister, are being helpful to Mommy.
>> You and Bruce are old enough now to work for peace. . . . I am fine. Happy birthday, Tom.
>> Love, Dad.
> Announcer: That was Walter Eugene Wilber, Commander, U.S. Navy, American pilot captured in the Democratic Republic of Vietnam, addressing his son on the occasion of his birthday.

14.   Special to the *New York Times*, "Laird Discounts P.O.W. Interviews," December 29, 1970; Christopher Lydon, "Camp Termed Showplace," *New York Times*, December 29, 1970.

15.   Hubbell, *P.O.W.*, 558. Hubbell provides no citation for the quote.

16.   Ibid., 558.

17. Ibid., 558–59.

18. See discussion on orders to take torture, not to make statements or write letters, in Stephen A. Rowan, *They Wouldn't Let Us Die: The Prisoners of War Tell Their Story* (Middle Village, NY: Jonathan David Publishers, 1973), 165.

19. Hubbell, *P.O.W.*, 559, 561.

20. Bill Zimmerman, *Troublemaker: A Memoir from the Front Lines of the Sixties* (New York: Doubleday, 2011), 249; NVN: *Ramsey Clark Visit to POW Camp*, Library of Congress POW/MIA Database and Documents, CIA Files, Reel 408, vol. 28, 35, http://lcweb2.loc.gov/frd/pwmia/405/100645.pdf; NVN: *Jane Fonda Meets With U.S. POWs in Hanoi*," Library of Congress POW/MIA Database and Documents, CIA Files, Reel 408, vol. 25, 12–14, http://lcweb2.loc.gov/frd/pwmia/408/119397.pdf.

21. Tom Wilber interview with Lynn Guenther, March 8, 2018.

22. *North Vietnam, pre-1975: Letter to Walter Cronkite of CBS News Regarding Bombings in the Democratic Republic of Vietnam,* Library of Congress POW/MIA Database and Documents, Senate Committee Source Data Files, Reel PDS88, http://lcweb2.loc.gov/frd/pwmia/PDS88/127954.pdf.

23. William Beecher, "Laird Discusses Released P.O.W.s," *New York Times*, September 12, 1972.

24. Copies of the tape and transcript are in the author's possession. Portions of the transcript have been edited for length and clarity.

25. Dick Baumbach "Wilber Silent on Charges," *Elmira Star-Gazette*, June 27, 1973; Hubbell, *P.O.W.*, 601–3.

26. Associated Press, "Navy Censures Former POWs for Misconduct," *Cornell Daily Sun*, September 28, 1973.

3. Profiles in Dissent: "The Peace Committee" of Enlisted POWs

1. Howes, *Voices of the Vietnam POWs*, 108. "The Eight," known as the Peace Committee, are also referred to as "PCs" by some historians.

2. Wilber and Miller were not part of the Peace Committee, there being no contact before the Paris Peace Accords were signed.

3. Guy as told to Grant, *Survivors*, 253–55.

4. Ibid., 211–12, 334.

5. Rochester and Kiley, *Honor Bound*, 268–69.

6. Daly. *Black Prisoner of War,* 50, 63.

7. Captain Floyd "Hal" Kushner was an Army doctor who was captured November 1968. Initially held and moved with ten South Vietnamese army prisoners, he arrived at the camp with other Americans in January 1968. There, and until the group reached Hanoi in spring 1971, he treated fellow captives using such rudimentary resources available. While he was held in Hanoi, his wife, Valerie, endorsed the antiwar

candidacy of George McGovern for president, a story used by filmmakers Ken Burns and Lynn Novick in their 2017 film *The Vietnam War*, to support a female-betrayal narrative for the loss of the war.

8. Daly refers to the site as Plantation Gardens. The "gardens" referred to a small mound in the courtyard planted with flowers. After three years of jungle-living and forty-eight days of rough travel on the Ho Chi Minh Trail, the basketball hoops in the courtyard and electric lighting in their rooms—not cells—the change was, wrote Daly in *Black Prisoner of War*, "like going from Hell to Heaven" (174). Elliott Gruner, *Prisoners of Culture: Representing the Vietnam POW* (New Brunswick, NJ: Rutgers University Press, 1993), contrasts Daly's description of Hanoi conditions with the majority of pilot memoirs that used "hell" to describe their experience.

9. Daly, *Black Prisoner of War*, 184. Although the Kushner group knew about the PCs and *New Life*, they were kept separated by the guards for several months. Dr. Kushner and Frank Anton, a warrant officer helicopter pilot, were moved to a holding area for officers.

10. Ibid., 186–87. In his memoir, Daly doubts that most of the letters ever made it out of Vietnam, speculating that they were "filed" for later use by prison authorities.

11. Ibid., 190, 194. Emphasis added.

12. Gruner, in *Prisoners of Culture*, refers to an "unsettling consecration of experience" in the memoirs "written by white male pilots" that then accounts for their supposed emergence from imprisonment as better men (149).

13. Daly, *Black Prisoner of War*, 10–12, 39. The Jehovah's Witnesses grew out of an antiwar group during the First World War known as The Bible Students, or the Russellites, named for Charles Russell, a Bible fundamentalist. In June 1918, the group's president and six other leaders were convicted under the federal Espionage Act and sentenced to twenty years in prison. In 1931, the group was renamed the Jehovah's Witnesses. Zoe Knox, "'A Greater Danger than a Division of the German Army': Bible Students and Opposition to War in World War I America," *Peace & Change: A Journal of Peace Research* (April 2019), 207–43.

14. Daly, *Black Prisoner of War*, 10–12.

15. Ibid., 1–4. The quoted words are Daly's, 4.

16. Ibid., 14.

17. Ibid., 40.

18. Ibid., 209.

19. The details of Chenoweth's background are compiled from Michael E. Ruane, "Traitors or Patriots? Eight Vietnam POWs Were Charged with Collaborating with the Enemy," *Washington Post*, September 22, 2017; and Chenoweth's correspondence with Lembcke, March 7, 2019.

20. See Rochester and Kiley, *Honor Bound,* 446, 456, for details on Portholes.

21. "Work" in the prison camps like Portholes meant foraging for food and water. The prisoners were sometimes lightly watched by guards and allowed some contact with one another and local villagers.

22. The details on Riate are taken from Jerry Lembcke, correspondence with Bob Chenoweth, March 14, 2019.

23. Riate's song in Vietnamese can be accessed on YouTube: https://www.youtube.com/watch?v=OLtc3YevH8o&feature=youtube.

24. Daly, *Black Prisoner of War,* 208. Daly continued, "As the raid went on, I was suddenly filled for the first time in my life with real hate. I hated every plane and every pilot who flew them. And I felt so sick at what was happening outside that window—so sick and ashamed and sad at what my country was doing—that I started to cry."

25. Daly, *Black Prisoner of War,* 208.

26. Xuan Oanh also asked the Peace Committee if they wanted to leave Hanoi interspersed with the other prisoners or as group. The Eight, aware of the potential threat, chose safety in numbers, remaining in their cell block and choosing to be released together for the March 16, 1973, flights from Hanoi. Tom Wilber interview with Bob Chenoweth, Hanoi, July 4, 2019.

27. Once stateside, Guy walked back his threats of violence against the dissidents. Howes, *Voices of the Vietnam POWs,* 109.

28. Zalin Grant, *Survivors* (New York: W. W. Norton, 1975), 210.

29. Ibid., 272.

30. Ibid., 275.

31. John Young also recalled making a tape for Christmas broadcast in 1968 that would let his family know he was alive, but it was never used. In July 1969, he was asked by an official to make an antiwar statement for broadcast, but he refused. Ibid., 274–76.

32. Ibid., 280–81.

33. Hubbell, *P.O.W.,* 505, 508–509. Hubbell attributes those reports of abuse to Dennis Thompson and Edward Leonard but does not say where, when, and to whom they claimed such.

34. Grant, *Survivors,* 276.

35. Ibid., 276.

36. Hubbell, *P.O.W.,* 567–68. Since *P.O.W.* is not footnoted, we don't know the source of the memo Hubbell refers to. By that time, however, in-service GIs and Vietnam veterans were making similar statements quite widely so there is no reason to question the general validity of his claim against Branch.

37. Grant, *Survivors,* 245–46.

38. Daly, *Black Prisoner of War,* 135.

39. Rochester and Kiley, *Honor Bound,* 457.

40. Hubbell, *P.O.W.*, 533. Again, without footnotes, we cannot know his source for this. It is noteworthy that the anecdote does not appear in Daly or Grant, which are the two best primary sources on Kavanaugh. Rochester and Kiley, who wrote their book twelve years after Hubbell, and rely on him for other details, do not repeat the story.
41. Grant, *Survivors*, 280–82.
42. Daly, *Black Prisoner of War*, 203–4.
43. Grant, *Survivors*, 317.
44. Ibid., 338.
45. Ibid., 338.
46. The Pentagon's press release is reproduced in ibid., 340.
47. Rochester and Kiley's remark is in *Honor Bound*'s page 563 footnote that has within it a set of citations to a chief of staff memo, and articles from the *New York Times* and *Washington Star & News*; Lieutenant Colonel Gary D. Solis, *U.S. Marine Corps, Marines and the Military Law in Vietnam: Trial by Fire* (Washington, DC: U.S. Marine Corps History and Museums Division, Headquarters, 1989), 218–19; Grant, *Survivors*, 334–43.
48. Daly, *Black Prisoner of War*, 265.
49. Silber was called before the House Un-American Activities Committee (HUAC) in the 1950s. He became famous for his edited collections of folk and political music, *Sing Out*, and *Folksinger's Workbook*. During the Vietnam War, he edited the widely read *National Guardian*, a newspaper that featured the work of Australian journalist Wilfred Burchett. Dane was a folk, blues, and jazz singer who performed with Muddy Waters, Memphis Slim, and Pete Seeger. According to Wikipedia, she was the first American musician to tour in post-revolutionary Cuba.
50. Chenoweth correspondence with Lembcke, March 5, 2019. According to Chenoweth, Riate was assassinated in 1984. He was thirty-nine.
51. In correspondence with Tom Wilber, July 16, 2018, Chenoweth recalls being told of Riate's assassination by his brother. Riate also worked with Indochina Peace Campaign (IPC), lending his words to an organizing poster that urged rejection of the SROs' claims of torture and called out the brutal treatment of prisoners by the U.S and Saigon forces. See Series III.ii, Folder 4 of the IPC files in Special Collections at the University of Massachusetts Library, Boston.

4. *The Manchurian Candidate* Stalks the Homeland: Hollywood Scripts the POW Narrative

1. Epigraph: Rochester and Kiley, *Honor Bound*, 562.
2. Among the studies debunking brainwashing was Robert Jay Lifton's 1961 *Thought Reform and The Psychology of Totalism: A Study of Brainwashing in China* (New York: W. W. Norton, 1961).
3. Remarkably, in early pages of *Honor Bound*, Rochester and Kiley cited a

reason for the Pentagon to drop the charges against the PCs, which was that they had acted with honor.

4. Risner, *The Passing of the Night: My Seven Years as a Prisoner of the North Vietnamese* (New York: Random House, 1973), 91–92.

5. There might be some historical interpolation in Howes's assessment of how seminal *The Manchurian Candidate* was in the myth-making that grew out of the Korean War POW experience and how influential it was on the pilots destined for Vietnam. In a 2003 recall of the film's history, critic Roger Ebert points out that it had only a two-year run, 1962 to 1964, and was not re-released until 1988. Its initial popularity, moreover, was due to its allegorical reference to the Kennedy assassination in 1963, more than what it said about the war in Korea. Ebert recalled being told by John Frankenheimer, the film's director, that Frank Sinatra, who starred in the film, "purchased the rights [to the film] and kept it out of release from 1964 to 1988 . . . [out of] remorse after Kennedy's death."

6. The 1954 *The Bamboo Prison*, out just a year after fighting ended in summer 1953, appears now as a shakedown cruise by a Hollywood unsure about what to do with the Korean War POW story. On the one hand, the film has throwback appeal to a Second World War film like *Stalag 17*, including the slapstick humor that would be the hallmark of the 1960s television series *Hogan's Heroes*. On the other hand, *Bamboo Prison* pioneers the themes of brainwashing and collaboration with the enemy that will lead to *The Manchurian Candidate* and dominate the POW genre from then on.

7. Elaine May, *Fortress America: How We Embraced Fear and Abandoned Democracy* (New York: Basic Books, 2017).

8. The interest of fliers and flight crews would have been heightened by depictions of pilots shot down and captured in Korea. But how many of those were there in the war? For his *Remembered Prisoners of a Forgotten War,* historian Lewis H. Carlson interviewed Robert Coury, who told of being shot down and captured in June of 1953. Coury recalled meeting three more captive pilots at an interrogation center. In the 1954 film *Bridges at Toko-Ri*, Navy Lieutenant Harry Brubaker, played by William Holden, is shot down but killed by enemy troops before capture. Based on a book by James Michener, with Grace Kelly and Mickey Rooney in supporting roles, the film was hugely popular. Lewis, Carlson, *Remembered Prisoners of a Forgotten War* (New York: St. Martin's Press, 2002), 35.

9. In his speech "The Ultimate Weapon" on communist mind control, former Major William Mayer, who was the primary source for Kinkead, said, "We thought we knew about the burning bamboo splints under the fingernails used by all Orientals." All the ordinary U.S. soldiers knew this, he said. But he went on to say that 95 percent of the men

saw no such physical abuse. https://www.usa-anti-communist.com/
pdf1/Mayer_Brainwashing_Ultimate_Weapon/Brainwashing_The_
Ultimate_Weapon-Major_William_E_Mayer-Oct4_1956.pdf

10. Paul Hanebrink, *A Specter Haunting Europe: The Myth of Judeo-Bolshevism* (Cambridge, MA: Belknap Press, 2019), writes the history of the racializing of anti-communism.

11. Vietnam War and Second World War captivities contrast in other ways. Germans, for example, followed the Geneva guidelines for treatment. Japan did not follow those guidelines and did murder some POWs. Notably, thousands of prisoners taken by Japan are thought to have died on ships sunk by U.S. submarines and air attacks.

12. The scenes of capture resemble those in the Second World War classic *Bridge On the River Kwai*, replete with the captives whistling a marching cadence, whereas the Viet Minh are portrayed as buffoonish as the Germans in *Stalag 17*.

13. In the film figure cut by Raspeguy, we can recognize a composite profile of the real-life Vietnam POWs Edison Miller and Gene Wilber—modest class background, affinity with the racial/ethnic Other, and aversity with military authority.

14. Hershberger, *Traveling to Vietnam*, 143–44.

15. George Smith's story is told by Howes in *Voices of the Vietnam POWs*.

16. Chapter 9 of Lembcke's *The Spitting Image: Myth, Memory, and the Legacy of Vietnam* (New York: New York University Press, 1998) uses archives from the Margret Herrick Library and director Waldo Salt's papers at the UCLA library to document the making of *Coming Home*.

17. A film proposed by Old Westbury College professor Steve Talbot in April 1973, titled *The Man in the Sky Is a Killer*, is illustrative of New Left attitudes of the POWs. The script describes POWs as "almost all loyal officers; they are career men, volunteers . . . who recall an America before all this trouble started. Like Cold War Rip Van Winkles, they praise the December [1972] bombing, and attack the people who were downing or bad-mouthing our government policies." Parenthetically, the proposal included a nod to a place in the film for the Peace Committee. The title of the film is said to be a Vietnamese saying.

18. The association of the American Left with global communism was taken seriously in prowar conservative circles during the war. See Hon. John G. Schmitz, *The Viet Cong Front in the United States*, read into the *Congressional Record*, April 21, 1971, as *The Second Front of the Vietnam War: Communist Subversion of the Peace Movement*. Schmitz was a congressman from Orange County, California, and a member of the John Birch Society.

19. See Hershberger, *Traveling to Vietnam*, for a full account of American antiwar delegations to Hanoi.

20. McEldowney's biographical details are taken from Suzanne Kelley

McCormack's Introduction to McEldowney's *Hanoi Journal, 1967,* which McCormack edited. The Rothstein details are from her interview with the PBS/WGBH series for *Peoples' Century,* "Young Blood: 1950–1975," https://www.pbs.org/wgbh/peoplescentury/episodes/youngblood /roth-steintranscript.html.

21. The other members of the Bratislava Hayden delegation were ERAP leader Rennie Davis, filmmaker Norman Fruchter, and Robert Allen and John "Jock" Brown, who joined the group in Bratislava.

22. McEldowney, *Hanoi Journal, 1967,* 58.

23. Ibid., 94–95.

24. After the meeting with Carrigan, Rothstein wrote: "I felt he was baiting and bullshitting us—because he wants to please the Vietnamese to get good treatment."

25. See Franklin's *M.I.A. or Mythmaking in America: How and Why the Belief in Live POWs Possessed a Nation* (New York: Lawrence Hill Books, 1992).

26. *When Hell Was in Session* (1979) was the first Vietnam POW-themed film. Set in the Hanoi prisons that the prisoners called "The Zoo" and "Alcatraz," it was based on Rear Admiral Jeremiah Denton's memoir of the same title. In a pseudo-documentary form, the film followed the chronology of Denton's shootdown, capture, interrogations, brutal treatment, isolation, Christian commitment, and release, with scenes interspersed of his family back home enduring his absence. The only characters in the film are Air Force and Navy pilots—officers. There is no hint of enlisted men among them or hint of divisions within the officer ranks.

27. Film critic Tony Williams in Malo and Williams, *Vietnam War Films,* reprised *Uncommon Valor,* attributing its production to, "The alliance of producer John Milius, an avowed right-wing militaristic Hollywood movie brat, and Ted Kotcheff, the director of *First Blood* that inaugurated the *Rambo* series." Jean-Jacques Malo and Tony Williams, *Vietnam War Films* (Jefferson, NC: McFarland & Company, 1994), 450.

28. See David Sirota, *Back to Our Future: How the 1980s Explains the World We Live In Now—Our Culture, Our Politics, Our Everything* (New York: Ballantine Books, 2011), for 1980s popular revisionist influences on public memory of the Vietnam War.

5. Damaged, Duped, and Left Behind

1. For a history of the coffeehouses see David L. Parsons in *Dangerous Grounds: Antiwar Coffeehouses and Military Dissent* (Chapel Hill: University of North Carolina Press, 2017); for GI Press history, see James Lewes, *Protest and Survive: Underground GI Newspapers during the Vietnam War* (New York: Praeger, 2003).

2. An Article 15 violation of the Uniform Code of Military Justice is heard in

an administrative proceeding for offenses akin to a misdemeanor in civilian law. An Article 15 guilty verdict is meted as nonjudicial punishment.

3. The military constraints on civilian reporters were tighter than sometimes believed today. It was not easy for reporters to get outside of major cities and military installations. When they did, they were sometimes "given a story" by a field unit's "public affairs liaison" and put on a plane back to Saigon. See David Cortright, *Soldiers in Revolt* (New York: Anchor Books, 1975), 269, for references to the Army's inquiries into dissent.

4. See Andrew Hunt, *The Turning: A History of Vietnam Veterans Against the War* (New York: New York University Press, 2001).

5. The University of Northern Colorado chapter of VVAW, of which Jerry Lembcke was a member, was banned from a Veterans Day parade in the early 1970s. Working around the ban, it followed behind the parade stepping to a solemn "death march" cadence.

6. For an analysis of Kerry's speech and responses to it, see John Kerry, *The New Soldier: Vietnam Veterans Against the War,* edited by David Thorne and George Butler (New York: Collier, 1971).

7. John R. Coyne, *The Impudent Snobs: Agnew vs. The Intellectual Establishment* (Arlington, VA: Arlington House Press, 1972).

8. Erving Goffman, *Stigma* (New York: Touchstone, 1964/1986).

9. See Daniel Ellsberg, *Secrets: A Memoir of Vietnam and the Pentagon Papers* (New York: Penguin, 2003).

10. The *Times* article was Jon Nordheimer, "Postwar Shock Besets Ex-G.I.s," *New York Times*, August 21, 1972; Peter Bourne, *Men, Stress, and Vietnam* (New York: Little, Brown, 1970).

11. The blackout of news about shot-down U.S. pilots may never have been as great as some Americans believe today. In Hubbell's *P.O.W.*, 51–52, he records pilot Larry Guarino's arrival in Hoa Lo prison in June of 1965 and telling Bob Peel, who had been captured earlier, that he had read about Peel's capture and that "your name has been officially released as definitely captured." Peel was the eighth pilot captured and a month later Guarino was the tenth.

12. The SROs also played the "buyout" card, offering Wilber and Miller the chance for "reinstatement" as commanding officers in the chain of command they had configured. See Rochester and Kiley, *Honor Bound*, 553.

13. The origins of the "weakness" theory in "official" accounts of Korean War POWs is in Albert D. Biderman, *March to Calumny: The Story of American POWs in the Korean War* (New York: Macmillan, 1963), 166–67.

14. Hubbell attributes the Kushners' motivations to "naivete, weakness, and mental illness," Hubbell, *P.O.W.*, 109. Rochester and Kiley add "lacked strength and intelligence and discipline" to the list, Rochester and Kiley, *Honor Bound*, 565.

15. See Seymour Hersh's coverage of the Wallace interview in "P.O.W. Who Made Antiwar Statements in Hanoi Recalls 'Pressure of Conscience,' " *New York Times*, April 2, 1973.

16. The *New York Times*, "Ex-P.O.W.s Cheer Nixon," May 23, 1970, made no mention of the dissidents, nor did its "400 Ex-P.O.W.s are Given $400,000 Dallas Reception," June 2, 1970. Tom Wilber, Gene's son, is a source for the behind-the-scenes shenanigans against the family.

17. Later determinations made it clear that the Code of Conduct was open to interpretation and was not law. Being unrelated to the Uniform Code of Military Justice, no legal determination can be made based on a dispute over whether a servicemember was following the Code of Conduct.

18. Rochester and Kiley, *Honor Bound*, 102, attribute the introduction of tap code as a means of communication to Air Force captain Carlyle Harris in the summer of 1965. Harris recalled learning about the tap code during a coffee break (not as part of the curriculum) when he was in Air Force survival training. A footnote in Rochester and Kiley dates the system back to the First World War and notes it was also used in Korean POW camps. The five-by-five matrix coded twenty-five letters of the alphabet, *K* being dropped and substituted with the letter *C*. John Dramesi characterizes the tap code as useful for "pornography and entertainment" in this 2008 interview: https://www.chicagoreader.com/Bleader/archives/2008/10/10/john-dramesis-unflattering-memories-of-his-fellow-pow-john-mccain.

19. Solis, *Trial by Fire*, 220.

20. "The two were retired with administrative letters of censure and in lasting disgrace." Rochester and Kiley, *Honor Bound*, 568.

21. As with other antiwar veterans, the diagnostic framing given their views functioned politically and culturally more than medically. Press reports at the time portrayed POWs as healthy, and later medical reports confirmed that. POW memoirs written as late as the mid-1980s make no mention of PTSD or trauma.

22. These details are taken from Franklin, *M.I.A.*, 39, 48–49. Photographs of the tiger cages were published in the July 17, 1970, *Life*. See Don Luce, "The Tiger Cages of Vietnam," www.historiansagainstwar.org/resources/torture/luce.html.

23. Jim Stockdale and Sybil Stockdale, *In Love and War*, rev. 1984 edition (Annapolis, MD: Naval Institute Press, 1990), 297–98. In a 1969 interview, John Frankenheimer, director of *The Manchurian Candidate*, told Canadian film critic Gerald Pratley: "We consulted every book written about brainwashing, and I remember reading one called *In Every War But One*. . . . We believed that we lived in a society that was brainwashed. And I wanted to do something about it." The interview can be accessed at https://www.filmsocietywellington.net.nz/db/screeningdetail.php?id=2.

24. Stockdale and Stockdale, *In Love and War*, 299–300.

25. Franklin, *M.I.A.*, 196n35.

26. Ibid., 13–23, for details on the counting of POWs, MIAs, and BNR. Bernie Rupinski, Gene Wilber's radar intercept officer and backseater, is an example of a flier known to have died in the 1968 shootdown but whose body

was not recovered. In 2015, Tom Wilber located Rupinski's gravesite in Thanh Chuong District, Nghe An Province, Vietnam. Based on Tom's findings, DPAA (Defense POW/MIA Accounting Agency) reopened the case (REFNO 1209) but as of 2021, the remains are still unrecovered.

27.   See L. C. McCollum, *History and Rhymes of the Lost Battalion*, (1919), and Arch Whitehouse, *Heroes and Legends of World War I* (New York: Doubleday, 1964) for more on the Legend of the Lost Command.

28.   Franklin, *M.I.A.*, 54. Franklin's description is from "Exhibit to Stir Opinion on P.O.W.s Opens in Capitol," *New York Times*, June 5, 1970.

29.   Ibid., 56–57.

30.   Tom Wilber has POW/MIA bracelets for Walter Eugene Wilber and Bernard Francis Rupinski. One with Gene Wilber's name was returned to Tom in 2015 by a woman who had purchased it in the early 1970s and had worn in through the return of the POWs.

31.   Franklin, *M.I.A.*, 5.

32.   Jeremy Kuzmarov and John Marciano. *The Russians are Coming, Again* (New York: Monthly Review Press, 2018), reviews that history and updates its relevance for current American obsessions with Russian influence in domestic politics.

33.   May's *Fortress America* delves into the social and cultural dimensions of the Cold War at home.

34.   Perot's remarks on McCain as reposted here can be found at the *Newsweek* online site: https://www.newsweek.com/ross-perot-slams-mccain-86763.

35.   Lembcke's *CNN's Tailwind Tale: Inside Vietnam's Last Great Myth* (Lantham, MD: Rowman & Littlefield, 2003) reveals the journalistic malfeasance and conspiratorial motif of the CNN report.

6. A Captive Nation: POWs as Grist for the American Myth

1.   Paul Boyer,. *When Time Shall Be No More: Prophecy Belief in Modern American Culture* (Cambridge, MA: Harvard University Press, 1992), 68–69. In 1629 John White implored his fellow colonists to support the venture in New England as "a bulwark against the Kingdom of Antichrist," and preacher Cotton Mather interpreted the colonists' war against the Indians (King Philip's War of 1675–1676) as a manifestation of the Red Horse of the Apocalypse foretold in the Book of Revelation. A century later, with the colonies nearing their final struggle for independence, the Christian prophets regaled their British oppressors as the Antichrist and warned that the Stamp Act could be the Mark of the Beast in disguise.

2.   Pauline Turner Strong. *Captive Selves, Captivating Others: The Politics and Poetics of Colonial American Captivity Narratives* (Boulder, CO: Westview Press, 1999), 48–51. The following paragraphs on the captivity narratives are indebted to Strong's book.

3.   Ibid., 52–55. The absence of any corroborative testimony for Smith's reprieve adds to the question about its accuracy.

4. Bruce Cumings, *North Korea: Another Country* (New York: New Press, 2004), 13. Cumings acknowledges Anderson, *Imagined Communities*, for his phrasing. Another defacing and widely used term was a one-letter abbreviation for Vietnamese, "the V." Jay Jensen, in *Six Years in Hell: A Returned Vietnam POW Views Captivity, Country, and the Future* (Orcutt, CA: Publications of Worth, 1974), uses that expression almost exclusively. Writing about the food, for example, he said, "The 'V' told us not to worry about the worms" (124).

5. Eugene B. McDaniel, *Before Honor: One Man's Spiritual Journey into the Darkness of a Communist Prison (Before Honor Is Humility—Proverbs 18:12)* (New York: A. J. Holman, 1975), 50; Larry Guarino, *A P.O.W.'s Story: 2801 Days in Hanoi* (New York: Ivy Books, 1990), 139; Ralph Gaither. *With God in a P.O.W. Camp*, 132.

6. Gaither, *With God in a P.O.W. Camp*, 128.

7. See memoirs by Larry Chesley, *Seven Years in Hanoi: A POW Tells His Story* (Salt Lake City: Bookcraft, 1973), 109; and Jensen, *Six Years in Hell*, 104, on the letter campaign. The letter campaign is central to the "official story": see John G. Hubbell, *P.O.W.*, 519. Craig Howes, in *Voices of the Vietnam POWs*, mentions the Amnesty International claim, 106. John McCain with Mark Salter, in *Faith of My Fathers* (New York: Random House, 1999), give credence to the post-Ho logic for the change, 290; as does former POW Phillip Butler in *Three Lives of a Warrior* (Scotts Valley, CA: CreateSpace, 2010), 331–32.

8. Another twist in the cycle wherein the confession to the SRO that the prisoner had given the interrogators something came to represent proof of having been tortured, was that the confession compelled the subordinate POWs to degrade themselves as "failures" before their own superiors. Excellent on this point is Howes, *Voices of the Vietnam POWs*, chapter 3.

9. Howes, *Voices of the Vietnam POWs*, 70, draws on Elaine Scarry, *The Body in Pain: The Making and Unmaking of the World* (New York: Oxford University Press, 1985), 85, to make a social-psychological point that, just as the warrior gives consent for the infliction of bodily pain when he joins the battle, prisoners at war give consent for torture.

10. Stockdale and Stockdale, *In Love and War*, 332–38.

11. Risner, *The Passing of the Night*, 117–21.

12. "Insisting on torture," wrote Howes, in *Voices of the Vietnam POWs*, "was thus the POWs' way of fighting the Vietnam War and of guaranteeing they would return home proudly as victors in 'the battle of Hanoi'" (70).

13. There is no doubt that the hardcore SROs thought that signs of physical damage to their bodies could be later translated into propaganda statements about the cruelty of the Communists. But their recognition that the same bodily damage could be represented as a statement

about *them* is an even more important insight into the prisoner-*at*-war mentality.

14. What Risner dismissed as "propaganda" can be read today to say more about his misunderstandings of the war than for anything about the North Vietnamese. In his memoir, *The Passing of the Night,* for example, he wrote: "They kept preaching to us [over the radio] that North Viet Nam had been tricked [by the Geneva agreement that had ended the French occupation of Vietnam]. To hear them tell it, the Vietnamese people had been guaranteed that they would be reunited, and that all they really wanted were free elections. We knew that was a lie. The story of the Communist takeover in North Viet Nam was a three-day blood bath in which they murdered five hundred of the top men in the country to pave the way for Communism. Their 'freedom-loving people' jazz did not pull the wool over our eyes" (143).

15. One of Salisbury's reports, "A Visitor to Hanoi Inspects Damage Laid to U.S. Raids," was carried on page 1 of the December 25, 1966, edition of the *New York Times.* Salisbury described Hanoi and included a map issued by the U.S. State Department listing military targets and juxtaposed it with the civilian sites said by Vietnamese to have been hit in recent raids. Salisbury's report had the standard journalistic qualifiers in all the right places: "the North Vietnamese say . . ." "four persons were reported killed . . ." "Hanoi residents certainly believe they were bombed. . . ."—On a personal note, I (Lembcke) acquired Salisbury's book, *Behind the Lines—Hanoi,* published in 1967, just before going to Vietnam in early 1969. As Stockdale may have feared, the book was, for me, an eye-opener that raised serious questions about the truth of U.S. government accounts of the bombing and what the war was all about.

16. Stockdale, *In Love and War,* 245–49.

17. Howes, *Voices of the Vietnam POWs,* 95.

18. Dunn's recollection is in Barbara Powers Wyatt, ed., *We Came Home,* 1977. Air Force Captain Joseph Crecca had a B.S. degree in mechanical engineering and wrote in Wyatt, *We Came Home,* that, while a prisoner, he "had the opportunity to study Russian as well as to teach mathematics, physics, classical music, and automobile theory and mechanics" (8).

7. The Heritage of Conscience: From the American War in Vietnam to America Today

1. Seymour M. Hersh, "The Scene of the Crime: A Reporter's Journey to My Lai and the Secrets of the Past," *The New Yorker,* March 22, 2015.

2. Matthew Breems, "Courage to Resist Vietnam Series Podcast, Episode 19: Susan Schnall," August 22, 2019.

3. VVAW's Winter Soldier hearing is documented in Andrew Hunt's 1999 *The Turning* and the 1972 film *Winter Soldier.* The IVAW hearing is

described by Nan Levinson in *War Is Not a Game: The New Antiwar Soldiers and the Movement They Built* (New Brunswick, NJ: Rutgers University Press, 2014), 2014.

4. Jon Krakauer, *Where Men Win Glory: The Odyssey of Pat Tillman* (New York: Anchor Books, 2010).

5. According to Krakauer, Tillman's friend Reka Cseresnyes contacted Chomsky on Tillman's behalf and the professor was open to meeting him (263–64).

6. Ibid., 329–41. Destruction of his belongings was against regulations. Tillman's status as a celebrity figure *cum* Army poster boy spawned resentment among his peers. Jason Porter, the NCO responsible for Tillman's orientation to Ranger training, thought of him as a "prima-donna football star" who other NCOs sucked up to. Porter was in the platoon that killed Tillman. Knowing as we do that high ranking officers who resented Gene Wilber's dissent green-lighted an assault on him, it is not conspiracist to imagine that Tillman's resentful peers sensed a wink-and-a-nod from their higher-ups to take him out.

7. More details on the differences between duty in Iraq and Vietnam can be found in Jerry Lembcke, *PTSD: Diagnosis and Identity in Post-Empire America* (Lanham, MD: Lexington Books, 2013), 59–65.

8. Military and veteran dissent in the years of the war in Vietnam went through phases of official denial/suppression, criminalizing, and pathologizing, as we see in the cycle experienced by the dissenting POWs. Outright suppression and criminalizing of in-service and veteran dissent during the wars in Iraq and Afghanistan, by contrast, skipped the first two phases and picked up where the Vietnam trajectory left off, treating dissent as a mental and emotional disorder, a.k.a. PTSD.

9. Joseph B. Verrengia, "Some Iraq Vets Find Forgetting the Hardest Part About Killing," Associated Press (April 18, 2003).

10. The *Pittsburgh Tribune-Review* published "Stress of Battle Haunts Soldiers" in February 2005, and *USA Today* also published a feature in October 2007. A *New York Times* series that began on the front page of a mid-January 2008 Sunday edition ran for 5,600 words across three full pages, and continued for several more days. In *PTSD: Diagnosis and Identity in Post-Empire America*, Lembcke took a phenomenological dive into the *Times* series to ferret out its meaning.

11. Inspired by the Coffeehouse Movement of the Vietnam War years, antiwar veterans of Iraq opened coffeehouses near Fort Hood, Texas; Fort Lewis, Washington; and Fort Drum, New York. Ending the U.S. occupation of Iraq was part of their mission, but the new coffeehouses functioned more as service centers offering mental health counseling and help with personal and family issues.

12. Lolita C. Baldor and Robert Burns, "Reinstate? Reassign? Navy to

Decide Fate of Fired Captain," *The Associated Press*, April 19, 2020; Lolita C. Baldor and Robert Burns, "Navy Recommends Reinstatement of Fired Carrier Captain," *The Associated Press*, April 25, 2020; Eric Schmitt and Helene Cooper, "Navy to Pursue Wider Inquiry Into Actions Taken on Ship Hit by Coronavirus," *New York Times*, April 30, 2020.

13.   https://www.usatoday.com/story/news/politics/2020/04/07/timeline-capt-crozier-firing-acting-navy-secretary-modly-resigning/2964617001/.

14.   An April 16, 2020, "open letter" in *The Nation* magazine signed by nearly 100 former members of Students for a Democratic Society (SDS) invoked the experience of post–World War 1 Germany for its lessons for the then-upcoming Trump-Biden presidential election: https://www.thenation.com/article/activism/letter-new-left-biden/. Historian Van Gosse averred that the reelection of Donald Trump in 2020 threatened a martializing of American political culture: https://organizingupgrade.com/an-illiberal-democracy-if-trump-wins-again/.

15.   Editorial, *New York Times*, May 18, 2020, https://www.nytimes.com/2020/05/18/opinion/trump-military.html.

SELECTED BIBLIOGRAPHY

Allen, Michael J. *Until the Last Man Comes Home: POWs, MIAs, and the Unending Vietnam War*, Chapel Hill: UNC Press, 2009.

Anton, Frank. *Why Didn't You Get Me Out? Betrayal in the Viet Cong Death Camps; The Truth About Heroes, Traitors, and Those Left Behind.* Arlington, TX: Summit, 1997.

Baumbach, Dick. "Wilber Silent on Charges," *Elmira Star-Gazette*, June 27, 1973.

Bates, Milton. *The Wars We Took to Vietnam: Cultural Conflict and Storytelling.* Berkeley: University of California Press, 1996.

Beecher, William. "Laird Discusses Released P.O.W.s." *New York Times*, September 28, 1972.

Biderman, Albert D. *March to Calumny: The Story of American POWs in the Korean War.* New York: Macmillan, 1963.

Blakey, Scott. *Prisoner at War: The Survival of Commander Richard A. Stratton.* Garden City, NY: Anchor Books, 1978.

Bourne, Peter. *Men, Stress, and Vietnam*. New York: Little, Brown, 1970.

Boyer, Paul. *When Time Shall Be No More: Prophecy Belief in Modern American Culture.* Cambridge, MA: Harvard University Press, 1992.

Breems, Matthew. "Courage to Resist Vietnam Series Podcast, Episode 19: Podcast Interview with Susan Schnall," August 22, 2019.

Browne, Malcolm. "Thousands Watch 67 Prisoners Depart." *New York Times*, March 30, 1973.

Burchett, Wilfred. *Mekong Upstream*. N/A: Red River Publishing House, 1957.

Chesley, Larry. *Seven Years in Hanoi: A POW Tells His Story*. Salt Lake City: Bookcraft, 1973.

Carlson, Lewis. *Remembered Prisoners of a Forgotten War*. New York: St. Martin's Press, 2002.

Chu Chí Thành, *Memories of the War*. Hanoi: Vietnam News Agency Publishing House, 2015.

Clements, Charles, M.D., *Witness to War: An American Doctor in El Salvador*. New York: Bantam Books, 1984.

Clinton, James W. *The Loyal Opposition: Americans in North Vietnam, 1965–1972*. Niwot, CO: University Press of Colorado, 1995.

Coffee, Gerald. *Beyond Survival: Building on Hard Times—A POW's Inspiring Story*. Aiea, Hawaii: Coffee Enterprises, Inc., 2013 (revised).

Condon, Richard. *The Manchurian Candidate*. New York: Orion, 2013 (reprint).

Cortright, David. *Soldiers in Revolt*. New York: Anchor Books, 1975.

Coyne, John R. *The Impudent Snobs: Agnew vs. The Intellectual Establishment*. Arlington, VA: Arlington House Press, 1972.

Cumings, Bruce. *North Korea: Another Country*. New York: New Press, 2004.

Daly, James A., and Lee Bergman. *Black Prisoner of War: A Conscientious Objector's Vietnam Memoir*. Lawrence: University Press of Kansas, 2000. First published in 1975 by Bobbs-Merrill, under the title *A Hero's Welcome*.

Denton, Jeremiah, and E. Brandt. *When Hell Was in Session*. Clover, SC: Commission Press, 1976.

Ehrlick, Darrel. "Interview with Rodney Knutson," *Gazette* (Billings, MT), November 11, 2015.

Ellsberg, Daniel. *Secrets: A Memoir of Vietnam and the Pentagon Papers*. New York: Penguin, 2003.

Franklin, H. Bruce. *M.I.A. or Mythmaking in America: How and Why the Belief in Live POWs Possessed a Nation*. New York: Lawrence Hill Books, 1992.

Gaither, Ralph. *With God in a P.O.W. Camp*. Nashville, TN: Broadman Press, 1973.

Goffman, Erving. *Stigma*. New York: Touchstone, 1964/1986.

Grant, Zalin. *Survivors*. New York: W. W. Norton, 1975.

Greene, Felix. *Vietnam! Vietnam!* Palo Alto, CA: Fulton Publishing Company, 1966.

Gruner, Elliott. *Prisoners of Culture: Representing the Vietnam POW*. New Brunswick, NJ: Rutgers University Press, 1993.

Guarino, Larry. *A P.O.W.'s Story: 2801 Days in Hanoi*. New York: Ivy Books, 1990.

Hanebrink, Paul. *A Specter Haunting Europe: The Myth of Judeo-Bolshevism*. Cambridge, MA: Belknap Press, 2019.

Hersh, Seymour M. "The Scene of the Crime: A Reporter's Journey to My Lai and the Secrets of the Past," *The New Yorker*, March 22, 2015.

———. "P.O.W. Who Made Antiwar Statements in Hanoi Recalls 'Pressure of Conscience,'" *New York Times*, April 2, 1973.

Hershberger, Mary. *Traveling to Vietnam: American Peace Activists and the War*. Syracuse, NY: Syracuse University Press, 1998.

Howes, Craig. *Voices of the Vietnam POWs: Witnesses to Their Fight*. New York: Oxford University Press, 1993.

Hubbell, John G. *P.O.W.: A Definitive History of the American Prisoner-of-War Experience in Vietnam, 1964–1973*. New York: Reader's Digest Press, 1976.

Hunt, Andrew. *The Turning: A History of Vietnam Veterans Against the War*. New York: New York University Press, 2001.

Jensen, Jay R. *Six Years in Hell: A Returned Vietnam POW Views Captivity, Country, and the Future*. Orcutt, CA: Publications of Worth, 1974.

Kerry, John. *The New Soldier: Vietnam Veterans against the War*. Edited by David Thorne and George Butler. New York: Collier, 1971.

Knox, Zoe. "A Greater Danger than a Division of the German Army: Bible Students and Opposition to War in World War I America," *Peace & Change* 44/2 (April 2019): 207–43.

Krakauer, Jon. *Where Men Win Glory: The Odyssey of Pat Tillman*. New York: Anchor Books, 2010.

Kuzmarov, Jeremy, and John Marciano. *The Russians are Coming, Again*. New York: Monthly Review Press, 2018.

Lembcke, Jerry. *PTSD: Diagnosis and Identity in Post-Empire America*. Lanham, MD: Lexington Books, 2013.

———. *CNN's Tailwind Tale: Inside Vietnam's Last Great Myth*. Lanham, MD: Rowman & Littlefield, 2003.

———. *The Spitting Image: Myth, Memory, and the Legacy of Vietnam*. New York: New York University Press, 1998.

Levinson, Nan. *War Is Not a Game: The New Antiwar Soldiers and the Movement they Built*. New Brunswick: Rutgers University Press, 2014.

Lewes, James. *Protest and Survive: Underground GI Newspapers during the Vietnam War*. New York: Praeger, 2003.

Lifton, Robert Jay. *Thought Reform and the Psychology of Totalism: A Study of Brainwashing in China*. New York: W. W. Norton, 1961.

Luce, Don, "The Tiger Cages of Viet Nam," www.historiansagainstwar.org/resources/torture/luce.html.

Lydon, Christopher. "Camp Termed Showplace," *New York Times*, December 29, 1970.

Lynd, Staughton, and Tom Hayden. *The Other Side*. New York: New American Library, 1966.

Malo, Jean-Jacques, and Tony Williams. *Vietnam War Films*. Jefferson, NC: McFarland & Company, 1994.

May, Elaine Tyler. *Fortress America: How We Embraced Fear and Abandoned Democracy*. New York: Basic Books, 2017.

McCain, John. *Faith of My Fathers*. With Mark Salter. New York: Random House, 1999.

McCollum, L. C. *History and Rhymes of the Lost Battalion*. N.p.: n.p., 1919.

McDaniel, Eugene B. *Before Honor: One Man's Spiritual Journey into the Darkness of a Communist Prison (Before Honor Is Humility— Proverbs 18:12)*. New York: A. J. Holman, 1975.

McEldowney, Carol Cohen. *Hanoi Journal, 1967*. Edited by Suzanne Kelley McCormack and Elizabeth R. Mock. Amherst: University of Massachusetts Press, 2007.

New York Times, "Laird Discounts P.O.W. Interviews," December 29, 1970.

New York Times, "Ex-P.O.W.s Cheer Nixon," May 23, 1970.

New York Times, "400 Ex-P.O.W.s are Given $400,000 Dallas Reception," June 2, 1970.

Nordheimer, Jon. "Postwar Shock Besets Ex-G.I.s," *New York Times*, August 21, 1972

O'Connor, Michael. *MiG Killers of Yankee Station*. Friendship, WI: New Past Press, 2003.

Parsons, David L. *Dangerous Grounds: Antiwar Coffeehouses and Military Dissent*. Chapel Hill: University of North Carolina Press, 2017.

Risner, Robinson. *The Passing of the Night: My Seven Years as a Prisoner of the North Vietnamese*. New York: Random House, 1973.

Rochester, Stuart, and Frederick Kiley. *Honor Bound: American Prisoners of War in Southeast Asia, 1961–1973*. Annapolis, MD: Naval Institute Press, 1999.

Ronco, Theo. "How American Pilots in North Vietnam Lived," *L'Humanité*, November 5, 1970.

Rowan, Stephen A. *They Wouldn't Let Us Die: The Prisoners of War Tell Their Story*. Middle Village, NY: Jonathan David Publishers, 1973.

Ruane, Michael E. "Traitors or Patriots? Eight Vietnam POWs Were Charged with Collaborating with the Enemy." *Washington Post*, September 22, 2017.

Salisbury, Harrison. *Behind the Lines: Hanoi*. New York: Harper & Row, 1967.

———. "A Visitor to Hanoi Inspects Damage Laid to U.S. Raids." *New York Times*, December 25, 1966.

Scarry, Elaine. *The Body in Pain: The Making and Unmaking of the World*. New York: Oxford University Press, 1985.

Silber, Irwin. *Folksinger's Wordbook*. N/A: Oak Publications, 1973.

Sirota, David. *Back to Our Future: How the 1980s Explains the World We Live In Now—Our Culture, Our Politics, Our Everything*. New York: Ballantine Books, 2011.

Smith, George E. *P.O.W.: Two Years with the Viet Cong*. Berkeley, CA: Ramparts Press, 1971.

Solis, Lieutenant Colonel Gary D. *U.S. Marine Corps, Marines and the Military Law in Vietnam: Trial by Fire*. Washington, DC: U.S. Marine Corps History and Museums Division, Headquarters, 1989.

Sonnez, Felicia. "Donald Trump on John McCain in 1999: 'Does being captured make you a hero?'" *Washington Post*, August 7, 2018.

Stockdale, Jim, and Sybil Stockdale. *In Love and War*. Rev. 1984 edition. Annapolis, MD: Naval Institute Press, 1990.

Strong, Pauline Turner. *Captive Selves, Captivating Others: The Politics and Poetics of Colonial American Captivity Narratives*. Boulder, CO: Westview Press, 1999.

Verrengia, Joseph B. "Some Iraq Veterans Find Forgetting the Hardest Part About Killing," Associated Press, April 18, 2003.

Whitehouse, Arch. *Heroes and Legends of World War I*. New York: Doubleday, 1964.

Wyatt, Barbara Powers, ed. *We Came Home*. Toluca Lake, CA: P.O.W. Publications, 1977.

Zaretsky, Natasha. *No Direction Home: The American Family and the Fear of National Decline*. Chapel Hill: University of North Carolina Press, 2007.

Zimmerman, Bill. *Troublemaker: A Memoir from the Front Lines of the Sixties*. New York: Doubleday, 2011.

Oral History Interviews
Conducted by Tom Wilber

Alvarez, Everett. April 26, 2019, Bethesda, Maryland
Beyer, Bruce. October 21, 2017, Arlington, Virginia
Bui Bac Van. January 12, 2015, Vinh, Vietnam
Burchett, George. March 4, 2018, and May 7, 2019, Hanoi
Butler, Phil. April 2018, telephone
Cash, Roy. March 8 and March 24, 2016, telephone
Chenoweth, Robert. June 26, 2017, telephone; November 29, 2017, Hanoi;
        February 22, 2018, Spokane, Washington; July 4, 2019, Hanoi
Chu Chi Thanh. October 29, 2016, Hanoi
Cunningham, Randy. October 4, 2018, Hanoi
Dodson, Max. February 11, 2017, Golden, Colorado
Dunleavy, Richard. January 28, 2016, telephone
Fant, Robert. March 18, 2016, telephone
Findley, Joseph. February 29, 2016, Maclean, Virginia
Gartley, Mark. February 19, 2019, telephone
Guenther, Lynn. March 9, 2018, telephone
Ha Quang Hung. August 12, 2016, Ho Chi Minh City, Vietnam
Jackson, Chuck. January 16, 2017, Hanoi; April 23, 2019, telephone
Kernan, Joe. September 24, 2018, telephone
Kuwatch, Scott. April 11, 2016, Middletown, Ohio
Le Do Huy. September 20, 2017, Hanoi
Le Khai. March 6 and May 2, 2018, Hanoi
Luu Van Hop. March 8, 2017, Hanoi
Maclear, Michael. March 22, 2016, telephone
Manlove, Don. August 11, 2015, telephone

Mather, Keith. March 8, 2018, Hanoi; August 16, 2019, Spokane,
    Washington
Miller, Edison. April 24, 2016, and July 5, 2018, Irvine, California
Nguyen Ba De. November 27, 2017, and March 4, 2018, Hanoi
Nguyen Bieu. September 19, 2017, and May 1, 2018, Hanoi
Nguyen Cong Thanh. November 14, 2014, Vinh, Vietnam
Nguyen Minh Y. April 4, 2017; January 29 and July 20, 2018; January 16 and
    18, May 6, July 4, and December 4, 2019, Hanoi
Nguyen Phong Nga. February 3, 2017, New York, New York
Nguyen Su. November 12, 2015. January 21, 2017, and December 5, 2019,
    Hanoi
Nguyen Sy Hung. March 28, 2016, Hanoi
Nguyen Tam Chien. May 2, 2018, Hanoi
Nguyen Thanh Quy. October 4, 2018, Hanoi
Nguyen Thi Binh. November 30, 2017, Hanoi
Nguyen Thi Binh A. January 25, 2018, Hanoi
Nguyen Thi Binh B. January 25, 2018, Hanoi
Nguyen Van Thu. May 16, 2015, Hanoi
Nguyen Van Coc. January 24 and 28, 2018, Hanoi
Nguyen Van Huynh. January 17, 2019, Hanoi
Nguyen Van Ninh. July 3, 2019, Hanoi
Nguyen Viet Bang. November 12, 2014, Vinh, Vietnam
Pham Phu Thai. March 26 and August 15, 2016, Hanoi
Pham Thi Vien. January 24, 2018, Hanoi
Rothstein, Vivian. January 7, 2019, telephone
Ryan, John. February 27, 2017, Morris Plains, New Jersey
Searcy, Chuck. June 13 and November 30, 2017; March 8, 2018, December
    7, 2019, Hanoi
Tạ Quoc Bao. May 18, 2016, Hanoi
Tong Tran Hoi. July 20, 2018, Hanoi
Tran Thi Dien Hong. August 12, 2016, Ho Chi Minh City, Vietnam
Tran Trọng Duyet. May 17, 2016, Haiphong, Vietnam; January 17, April 5,
    and November 27, 2017, and July 2, 2019, Hanoi
Truong Sinh. January 29, 2018, Hanoi
Vo Dien Bien. March 4, 2018, Hanoi
Weiss, Cora. October 17, 2017, December 17, 2018, March 11, 2019, New
    York, New York
Weiss, Peter. February 14, 2019, New York, New York
Zimmerman, Bill. April 12, 2019, telephone

Filmography

MOVIES

The Bamboo Prison	1954
Blood of Ghastly Horror	1967
The Bridge on the River Kwai	1957
The Bridges at Toko-Ri	1954
Cat on a Hot Tin Roof	1958
Coming Home	1978
Dragonfly Squadron	1954
First Blood	1982
Fixed Bayonets	1951
The Fog of War	2003
The Forgotten Man	1971
Good Guys Wear Black	1978
The Hanoi Hilton	1987
Jarhead	2005
The Lost Command	1966
Madame Curie	1943
The Manchurian Candidate	1962
Motorpsycho	1965
Mr. Majestyk	1973
Mrs. Miniver	1942
The Rack	1956
Rambo: First Blood Part II	1985
Rolling Thunder	1977
Ruckus	1980

Sir! No Sir!	2005
Some Kind of Hero	1982
Stalag 17	1953
Time Limit	1957
Uncommon Valor	1983
The Vietnam War	2017
Welcome Home Johnny Bristol	1971
When Hell Was in Session	1979
The Wild One	1953

TELEVISION

Hogan's Heroes
Jane Fonda in Five Acts
Lassie
South Park
Team America

Archival Collections

Schlesinger Library on the History of Women in America, Radcliffe
    Institute for Advanced Study, Harvard University
Swarthmore College Peace Collection, Swarthmore College
University Archives and Special Collections, Joseph P. Healey Library,
    University of Massachusetts Boston
Vanderbilt Television News Archive, Jean and Alexander Heard Libraries,
    Vanderbilt University
The Vietnam Center & Sam Johnson Vietnam Archive (VNCA), Texas Tech
    University
The Vietnam-Era Prisoner-of-War/Missing-in-Action Database, Library of
    Congress
Veterans History Project, American Folklife Center, Library of Congress

Index

Lightning Source UK Ltd.
Milton Keynes UK
UKHW012242220621
385978UK00003B/68